Pocket Guide to APA Style

Robert Perrin
Indiana State University

HOUGHTON MIFFLIN COMPANY
Boston   New York

Editor in chief: Patricia A. Coryell
Senior sponsoring editor: Suzanne Phelps Weir
Editorial associate: Bruce Cantley
Editorial assistant: Becky Wong
Senior project editor: Rosemary Winfield
Editorial assistant: Marlowe Shaeffer
Production/design coordinator: Bethany Schlegel
Senior manufacturing coordinator: Priscilla Bailey
Senior marketing manager: Cindy Graff-Cohen

Cover photo: Zefa Zeitgeist/Photonica

Printed in the U.S.A.

Library of Congress Control Number: 2002109656

ISBN: 0-618-30820-2

3456789-QUE-07 06 05 04

Contents

Contents

Preface

When students write papers for courses in any of the social or behavioral sciences—such as anthropology, psychology, sociology, or speech pathology—their instructors invariably ask them to follow the format and style guidelines created by the American Psychological Association (APA). First published in 1967 and most recently updated in 2001, the Association's *Publication Manual of the American Psychological Association* is a model of comprehensiveness: it ensures that writers present information to their readers in a clear and consistent manner.

Pocket Guide to APA Style is designed for students who need to write, document, and present papers in American Psychological Association style. This convenient and easy-to-use guide draws on the principles described in the fifth edition of the *Publication Manual of the American Psychological Association*. What sets *Pocket Guide to APA Style* apart from that lengthy manual is its overriding goal: this text presents the principles in a brief, yet complete and easy-to-use manner. The guide is ideal for undergraduates who are working with APA style for the first time. Yet graduate students and working professionals will also appreciate its user-friendliness. To enhance use, *Pocket Guide to APA* incorporates these helpful features:

- *Handbook Format*   To make information easy to find, *Pocket Guide* presents major principles in each chapter as numbered precepts (statements of key ideas).

- *Student Focus*   Clear explanations and numerous examples make *Pocket Guide* a convenient resource for upper-division undergraduates and beginning graduate students.

- *Writing Scholarly Papers: An Overview*   *Pocket Guide's* introductory chapter describes basic researching and writing methods, serving as a brief review.

- *Manuscript Preparation*   In one coherent chapter, *Pocket Guide* describes and illustrates all elements of an APA manuscript.

- *Editorial Style*   In one convenient chapter, *Pocket Guide* explains APA guidelines for punctuation and mechanics (periods, quotation marks, capitalization, number style, and so on), general writing style (transitions, verb tense, and so on), and word choice (jargon, biased language, and so on).

- *Separate Documentation Chapters* For easy use, *Pocket Guide* provides separate chapters to explain reference-list entries for periodicals, books, audiovisual sources, and electronic sources.

- *Reference-List Entries and In-Text Citations* 142 separate reference entries illustrate the principles of documentation in *Pocket Guide;* most entries are followed by corresponding in-text citations.

- *Tables, Charts, and Textboxes* Throughout *Pocket Guide,* tables, charts, and textboxes present material in easy-to-review formats.

- *Sample Papers* Two complete sample papers are included in *Pocket Guide,* one argumentative and one experimental; both have annotations related to manuscript form and issues of writing.

- *Discussion of Plagiarism* With its student focus, *Pocket Guide* includes a discussion of plagiarism and ways to avoid it.

- *Poster Presentations* In an appendix, *Pocket Guide* describes effective ways to prepare poster presentations.

ACKNOWLEDGMENTS

My work on *Pocket Guide* was made pleasant and productive because of the supportive, knowledgeable staff at Houghton Mifflin. I especially appreciate Suzanne Phelps Weir's commitment to this project, Bruce Cantley's enthusiastic and informed editorial assistance, and Rosemary Winfield's smooth handling of production work.

I am also indebted to the following people for their thoughtful reviews of the manuscript of *Pocket Guide to APA:*

Beverly L. Bower, Florida State University

Jake Harwood, University of Arizona

Betty Ayotte Jensen, Humboldt State University

Gretchen Kambe, University of Nevada, Las Vegas

Michelle Merwin, University of Tennessee at Martin

Denise A. Tucker, Florida State University

Karen M. Watt, University of Texas Pan American

Finally, I wish to thank Judy, Chris, and Jenny for their patience and encouragement.

R. P.

1   Writing Scholarly Papers

The research process is a complex combination of thinking, searching, reading, evaluating, writing, and revising. It is, in many ways, a highly personal process because writers approach research activities by drawing on different skills and past experiences. Yet researchers often follow a series of connected phases (which nonetheless occur in a different order for different people).

This chapter reviews, in a brief way, the common steps that most researchers go through; if you are an experienced researcher, you can use this chapter as a "refresher." If your research experiences are limited, consider each discussion carefully as you proceed with your work.

1a   Subject and Topic

Research begins with a subject. In some academic contexts, you may choose the subject yourself, usually with the instructor's approval. But in other contexts, you may be required to choose from a small number of topics or be assigned a topic with a predetermined focus.

GUIDELINES FOR ASSESSING GENERAL SUBJECTS

As you select potential subjects for your research (broad categories such as migrant education, test anxiety, the effects of divorce, and so on), keep these important and practical principles in mind:

- *Interest.* When possible, select a subject that interests you. Do not spend time researching a subject that does not make you curious.
- *Length.* Select a subject that can be adequately treated given the length requirements of the assignment. You may have to expand or reduce the scope of your subject to match these length constraints.
- *Materials.* Select a subject for which you can find materials of the kind spelled out in the assignment. Be aware that you can use libraries other than your own for your research and that the Internet provides access to a broad range of materials, both traditional and nontraditional.

- *Challenge.*   Select a subject that challenges you but that does not require technical or other specialized knowledge you may not have time to acquire.
- *Uniqueness.*   Select a subject that is not overused. Overly familiar subjects create little interest, and materials are soon depleted.
- *Perspective.*   Select a subject you can approach in a fresh, interesting way. Readers will appreciate your efforts to examine subjects in new ways.

NARROW TOPIC

In most instances, you need to narrow your large subject (migrant education, for example) to a specific topic (migrant education in Texas) so that you can both research selectively and address an issue in a focused way.

To discover ways in which to narrow a broad subject to a specific topic, skim general reference materials, paying particular attention to recurrent themes, details, and ideas. Then consider establishing a focus using selected strategies for limiting topics:

- *Time.*   Restrict the subject to a specific, manageable time span. For example: School violence in the 1950s.
- *Place.*   Restrict the subject to a specific location. For example: Teen pregnancy in rural areas.
- *Special circumstance.*   Restrict the subject to a specific context or circumstance. For example: Achievement testing for college admissions.
- *Specific population.*   Restrict the subject to address its effects on a selected group of people. For example: Skin cancer among elderly people.

1b   Thesis Statements, Hypotheses, or Stated Objectives

To clarify the central goal of your writing, present your ideas in one of three alternative ways.

THESIS STATEMENT

A thesis statement, sometimes called a problem statement, is a declarative statement (usually one but sometimes two or more sentences) that clarifies your specific topic, presents your opinion of (not merely facts about) the topic, and incorporates qualifications or limitations necessary to understand your views.

> Although the effects of birth order are always evident to some degree, other variables also affect personality, intelligence, and socialization.

HYPOTHESIS

A hypothesis is a conjectural statement that guides an argument or investigation; it can be explored (and potentially proved or disproved) by examining data related to your topic. Conditional in nature, a hypothesis is a statement to be assessed using available information.

> Students who delay work on major research projects until the last week are more likely to plagiarize than are students who begin their work early.

STATED OBJECTIVE

A stated objective is a brief, well-focused statement that describes a research paper that presents information. An objective statement is unsubtle and not arguable, but it must define the topic clearly and narrow the topic when necessary.

> I will share a brief history of polio in the United States, ranging from early epidemics to the last recorded American case.

1c   Research Goals

Although most research is prompted by specific academic or job-related requirements, you should also think broadly about the goals for your work—recognizing that research provides multifaceted learning experiences.

COURSE-RELATED GOALS

Course-related goals arc broad in nature and establish the foundation of your research work.

- *Using the library.*   Library-based research should take advantage of a full range of sources—and the electronic means to locate them. (See pages 5–8.)

- *Using the Internet for academic purposes.*   Research requires that you learn to use the Internet selectively for scholarly purposes, which means learning to evaluate the credibility and value of online materials. (See pages 8–9 and 11–12.)

- *Assessing source materials.*   In a global way, research depends on evaluating materials critically to ensure that you use sources that credibly support your ideas. (See pages 9–13.)

- *Taking notes.*   Research requires you to record ideas and information from your sources carefully and completely so that you can use them appropriately in your writing. (See pages 13–15.)

- *Responding effectively to opposing views.*   Fair-minded research acknowledges and uses opposing views to create balance in writing.

- *Synthesizing ideas.*   Effective research blends information and ideas from a variety of sources, thereby creating a comprehensive presentation that is, in some way, better or fairer or clearer than the presentation in individual sources.

- *Incorporating material into writing.*   Effective research leads to writing that incorporates ideas and information with clarity, accuracy, and style. (See pages 20–24 and 68–71.)

- *Citing sources accurately.*   Research requires that you give proper credit to the people whose ideas and information you have used; this technically focused process requires attention to detail. (See chapters 4–8.)

PROFESSIONAL GOALS

Professional goals develop from the process of establishing a working knowledge in your field of study. As such, they focus on specific skills and knowledge.

- *Learning to use specific sources.*   Research in each discipline requires familiarity with selected sources that are respected and commonly used.

- *Using specialized formats.*   Each discipline's research incorporates unique formats that you must learn to follow.

- *Using specialized writing styles.* Research in each discipline depends on specific stylistic patterns for presenting ideas and information.
- *Demonstrating discipline-specific knowledge.* Research in each discipline builds upon accepted information that you must be able to incorporate fluently.

PERSONAL GOALS

Personal goals concentrate on degrees of knowledge, improvement, sophistication, and experience. Although they are less easily quantified than goals matched to courses, they are equally important.

- *Learning about a subject.* Exploring a subject through research improves your understanding of your chosen discipline.
- *Improving skills.* Current research gives you the opportunity not only to use your early research work but also to develop more sophisticated skills.
- *Expanding experiences.* Research work allows for varied kinds of personal growth.

1d Research Methods

Methods of research vary depending on the project, but most projects require multidimensional work with a variety of sources. To complete such projects, take advantage of a full range of strategies.

LIBRARY-BASED RESEARCH

Learn to use all of the features of your library, especially familiarizing yourself with the research areas that you will most commonly use:

- *Reference:* The collection of general source materials—dictionaries, fact books, encyclopedias, indexes, guides, bibliographies, and so on—that can guide your preliminary research
- *Catalog (computer):* The cluster of computers where you secure the informational records of library materials

- *Stacks:* The bookcases where print materials (books, bound periodicals, and so on) are stored according to a classification system
- *Current periodicals:* The collection of recent copies of journals, magazines, and newspapers
- *Government documents:* The collection of printed materials from national, state, and local government departments and agencies—books, monographs, pamphlets, reports, and so on
- *Microforms:* The collection of microfilm and microfiche materials
- *Media:* The collection of audiovisual sources—films, videos, DVDs, CDs, and so on
- *New books:* The area where new books are displayed before being placed in the general collection
- *Special collections:* The area where rare books, archival materials, and other special materials are located
- *Special libraries:* The discipline-specific collections that are housed in sublibraries

ELECTRONIC SEARCH SYSTEMS AND PERIODICAL DATABASES

Electronic search systems (online "card catalogs") allow you to gather technical information about books, monographs, government documents, and other materials in the library's collection; periodical databases (online "indexes") allow you to gather technical information about—and very often secure full texts of—articles in journals, magazines, and newspapers. Both electronic search systems and periodical databases provide access to descriptive material about sources when using keyword search techniques.

Keyword searching uses easily recognizable words and phrases (often in combination) to access sources. Computer systems search for keywords in titles, tables of contents, and other descriptive source information and then display "matches." Use alternative phrases (*collaborative learning, group projects, collaboration, team research,* and so on) as you conduct your searches to locate a broad range of materials. Also explore Library of Congress listings—which are available online at most libraries—to discover unique category descriptions. For example, the Library of Congress system does not use the fairly conventional expression *medical ethics;* rather, its category notation is *medicine—moral and ethical aspects.*

Information About Books (and Other Library-Based Materials)

All electronic catalogs provide standardized information about each source in the library's collection:

- *Author:*   The full name of the author or authors
- *Title:*   The selection's full title, including subtitles
- *Facts of publication:*   The city, publisher, and copyright date
- *Technical description:*   Specific features—number of pages, book size, and so on
- *Location:*   The location of the source in the library's collection or in a special library or collection
- *Call number:*   The classification number assigned to the source (indicating where the source is located in the collection)
- *Number of items:*   The number of items, if more than one exists
- *Status:*   Information on whether the source is checked out, on reserve, on loan, and so on
- *Editions:* Descriptions of editions (second, third, revised, enlarged)
- *Notes:*   Descriptions of special features (bibliography, index, appendixes, and so on)
- *Table of contents:*   A listing of chapters and section titles and subtitles
- *Subject classification:*   The Library of Congress classification, both primary and secondary

Information About Periodicals

Periodical databases provide standardized information about articles in journals, magazines, and newspapers. They also provide articles in a variety of formats.

- *Article title:* The article's full title and subtitle (listed first because some articles have no attributed author)
- *Author:*   The full name of the author (or authors)

- *Periodical title:* The title of the journal, magazine, or newspaper
- *City:* The city of publication
- *Date:* The month/year, day/month/year, or season/year of publication
- *Volume and issue number:* The volume (which indicates the number of years that a periodical has been published) and number (which indicates the numbers of issues published each year) for journals and magazines, but not newspapers
- *Start page:* The page on which the article begins
- *Number of pages:* The article's total number of pages (in the original print format)
- *Formats for articles:* The formats available for selected articles: citation/abstract, full text, page image (See below.)

Format Options (Within a Periodical Database)

- *Citation/abstract:* Technical information, plus an abstract (brief summary of the ideas in an article)
- *Full text:* Technical information and abstract, plus the full text of an article in typed form
- *Page image:* Technical information and abstract, plus scanned images of an article as it appeared in the periodical

---

INTERNET-BASED RESEARCH

Your Internet search may lead you to a scholarly project (a university-based, scholarly site that makes a wide range of materials—such as full-text books, research data, and visual materials—available to researchers), an information database (a site that makes statistical information from governmental agencies, research institutions, or nonprofit corporations available to researchers), or a Web site (a site designed to share information, forward a political agenda, promote a product, advocate a position, or share ideas).

To navigate an Internet site successfully—and to gather crucial information for a reference-list entry—learn about the key elements of an Internet home page:

- *Electronic address (URL):* The "universal resource locator"—the combination of elements that locate the source (for example, http://www.aagpgpa.org/ is the URL for the American Association for Geriatric Psychology's Web site)
- *Official title:* The title and subtitle of the site
- *Author, host, editor, or Web master:* The name of the person (or people) responsible for the development and maintenance of the site
- *Affiliation or sponsorship:* The person, group, organization, or agency that develops and maintains the material on the site
- *Location:* The place (city, school, organization, agency, and so on) where the site originates
- *Posting date or update:* The date on which the site was first posted or the date of its most recent update (revision)
- *"About This Site":* A description of how the site was developed, a rationale for it, or information about those involved with the site
- *Site directory:* An electronic table of contents for the site

1e Evaluating Sources

Because all sources are not equally useful, you should analyze them and select the best ones. This ongoing process requires continued assessments and reassessments.

PRINT SOURCES

Print sources—journals, magazines, newspapers, books, and others—have traditionally been the mainstay of most research. Consequently, they are the easiest to evaluate because of their familiarity.

- *Author's credentials.* Determine whether an author's academic degrees, scholarly training, affiliations, or other published work establish his or her authority.

- *Appropriate focus.* Determine whether the source addresses the topic in a way that matches your emphasis.

- *Sufficient coverage.* Determine whether the source sufficiently covers the topic by examining its table of contents, reviewing the index, and skimming a portion of the text.

- *Reputable publisher.* University, academic, or trade presses publish most of the books you will use, which generally ensures their credibility. In addition, publishers often specialize in books related to particular subjects.

- *Publication date.* For many topics, sources more than ten or fifteen years old have limited value. However, consider creating a historical context by using old sources.

- *Respected periodicals.* Generally, you should use journals with strong organizational affiliations; furthermore, note that peer-reviewed journals (those that publish works only after they have been recommended by a panel of expert reviewers) offer more credibility than non–peer-reviewed journals. Choose specialized, rather than general-interest, magazines. Choose major newspapers for topics of international or national importance, but choose regional or local newspapers for issues of regional or local importance.

- *Useful supplementary materials.* Look for in-text illustrations, tables, charts, graphs, diagrams, bibliographies, case studies, or collections of additional readings.

- *Appropriate writing style.* Skim a potential source to see how it is developed (with examples, facts, narration, or description); also consider whether the author's style is varied, lively, and interesting.

AUDIOVISUAL SOURCES

Because of the range of audiovisual sources, you need to assess each kind individually using individual criteria. Nevertheless, many of the techniques employed for evaluating these sources correspond to those used with print and Internet sources.

- *Lectures and speeches.* Use criteria similar to those for print sources: speaker, relationship to your topic, coverage, sponsoring group or organization, and date.

- *Works of art, photographs, cartoons, and recordings.* Because these sources are used primarily to create interest in most researched papers, consider how well the image or performance illuminates the topic.

- *Maps, graphs, tables, and charts.* Evaluate these visual sources as you would traditional print sources.
- *Film, television, and radio.* When these sources serve informative purposes, evaluate them as you would print sources; when they are used creatively, evaluate them as you would art and other creative audiovisual forms.

INTERNET SOURCES

Although Internet sources provide a fascinating array of materials, much of what is posted on the Internet has not been subjected to scholarly review and is, therefore, not always credible. As a result, you should use only those Internet sources that meet important evaluative criteria:

- *Author, editor, host, or Web master's credentials.* A Web site may or may not have an author, editor, host, or Web master. If it does, explore the site for information about his or her credentials or qualifications to discuss the topic.

- *Appropriate focus.* Skim the Web site to see whether its focus is suitable for your topic. Sometimes the Web site's title makes the focus clear; at other times, an entire Web site has a general focus, but its internal links allow you to locate material on a narrower aspect of the larger subject.

- *Sufficient coverage.* Review documents in the Web site to see whether the coverage is thorough enough for your purposes.

- *Domains.* Examine the Web site's electronic address (URL) to see how the site is registered with the Internet Corporation for Assigned Names and Numbers (ICANN). The following common "top-level domains" provide useful clues about a Web site's focus and function:

.com	A commercial site. The primary function of a commercial site is to make money.
.edu	A site affiliated with an educational institution.
.gov	A government site. These sites present trustworthy information (statistics, facts, reports) and less useful interpretive materials.

.mil	A military site. The technical information on these sites is consistently useful, but interpretive material tends to justify a single, pro-military position.
.museum	A site for a museum. Because museums can be either nonprofit or for-profit institutions, consider the purpose that the particular museum serves.
.org	An organizational site. Because organizations seek to advance political, social, financial, educational, and other specific agendas, review these materials with care.

- Do not automatically discount or overvalue what you find on any particular kind of Web site. Rather, consider the biases that might influence the ways in which the information on a site is presented and interpreted.

- *Affiliation or sponsorship.* Examine the site to see whether it has an affiliation or a sponsorship beyond what is suggested by the site's domain.

- *Posting or revision date.* Identify the date of original posting or the date on which information was updated. Because currency is one of the benefits of Internet sources, look for sites that provide recent information.

- *Documentation.* Review Internet materials to see how thoroughly authors have documented their information. If facts, statistics, and other technical information are not documented appropriately, the information may be questionable as well.

- *Links to or from other sites.* Consider the "referral quality" that Internet links provide.

- *Appropriate writing style.* Skim the Web site to see how it is written. All sources do not, of course, have to be written in the same style, but it is an issue worth considering when you evaluate a source.

COMBINATIONS OF SOURCES

Although you must first evaluate your sources individually—whether they are print, audiovisual, or Internet— your goal is to gather a set of high-quality sources that together provide a balanced treatment of your topic. Consider these issues:

- *Alternative perspectives.* Taken collectively, does the work of your authors provide a range of perspectives — academic and popular, liberal and conservative, theoretical and practical, current and classical?

- *Varied publication, release, or distribution dates.* Does your group of sources represent the information, ideas, and interpretations of different periods?

- *Different approaches to the topic.* In combination, your sources should range from the technical (including facts and statistics) to the interpretive (providing commentary and assessments).

- *Diversity of sources.* Incorporate in your work a wide range of sources — periodicals, books, audiovisual sources, and electronic sources — to ensure that you have taken advantage of the strengths of each kind of source. Be aware, however, that in some instances your research must focus on selected kinds of sources.

Evaluating sources is an inexact process. No matter how carefully you review materials, some may later prove unhelpful. Yet early efforts to evaluate sources generally make later, more comprehensive work — reading and taking notes from the sources — more clearly focused and productive than it otherwise would be.

1f Note-Taking

Note-taking is a personal process, because different researchers prefer different methods for recording information and ideas from sources. However, all note-taking should be meticulous and consistent both to avoid plagiarism and to simplify the subsequent writing of the paper. Consider alternative methods for note-taking and remember that note-taking must be complete, consistent, matched to the kind of material being used, and honest.

Before taking notes from a source, create a complete and accurate entry for the reference list. See chapters 4–8 for general guidelines and samples.

METHODS OF NOTE-TAKING

Before beginning your note-taking, analyze each note-taking system and choose the one best suited to your specific project, library facilities, work habits, and instructor's expectations.

- *Note cards.* Note cards are easy to handle and rearrange during planning stages, but they hold only limited amounts of information.
- *Paper.* Paper is easy to handle and has sufficient room for copious notes, but notes on paper are difficult to organize during planning stages.
- *Computers.* Notes on computers do not have to be retyped during the writing process and can be printed multiple times, but on-site note-taking with computers is sometimes awkward.
- *Photocopies and printed texts.* Photocopied and printed materials do not have to be recopied, and they can be marked on. However, photocopying and printing can be expensive.

COMPLETE INFORMATION

Record complete identifying information with each separate note to avoid having to return to a source at a later — and potentially less convenient — time.

- *Author's name.* Record the author's last name (and first initial, if necessary for clarity); for multi-author sources, record only as many names as are necessary for clarity.
- *Title.* Record only key words from titles but use italics or quotation marks as appropriate.
- *Category notation.* Provide a brief descriptive term to indicate the idea or subtopic that the information supports.
- *Page numbers.* Record the page number(s) from which you gathered information. If material comes from several pages, indicate where the page break occurs. (A double slash [//] is a useful way to indicate a page break.)

CONSISTENT FORMAT

Record notes in a consistent format to avoid confusion at later stages of research and writing.

- *Placement of information.* Establish a consistent pattern for placing information so that nothing is omitted accidentally.

- *Abbreviations.* Use abbreviations selectively to save time and space, but use only standard abbreviations to avoid possible confusion later.
- *Notations.* Note anything unique about the source (for example, no page numbers in a pamphlet or an especially good chart).

KINDS OF NOTES

Four common kinds of notes serve most research purposes. Choose among these kinds of note-taking patterns depending on the sources you use.

- *Facts.* A fact note records technical information—names, dates, amounts, percentages—in minimal form. Record words, phrases, and information in a simple outline or list format and double-check the fact note for accuracy.
- *Summaries.* A summary note presents the substance of a passage in condensed form. After reading original material carefully, write a summary without looking at the original; this will ensure that the phrasing is yours, not the author's. Double-check the summary note to make sure that your wording is distinct from the original.
- *Paraphrases.* A paraphrase note restates the ideas from a passage in your own words but uses approximately the same number of words. Write a paraphrase without looking at the original, and then double-check the paraphrase note to make sure that the phrasing is yours.
- *Quotations.* A quotation note reproduces a writer's work *exactly.* Double-check the quotation note against the original; the copy must be an *exact* transcription of the original wording, capitalization, punctuation, and other elements.

1g Plagiarism

Plagiarism is the use of someone else's words, ideas, or line of thought without acknowledgment. Even when it is inadvertent—the result of careless note-taking, punctuating, or documenting—the writer is still at fault for dishonest work, and the paper will be unacceptable. You will remember the seriousness of the offense of plagiarism, and work to avoid committing it, when you remember that the word *plagiarism* comes from the Latin for "kidnapping." To avoid plagiarizing, learn to recognize distinctive content and expression in source materials and take accurate, carefully punctuated and documented notes.

COMMON KNOWLEDGE

Some kinds of information—facts and interpretations—are known by many people and are consequently described as **common knowledge.** That Alzheimer's disease is the leading cause of dementia in elderly people is widely known, as is the more interpretative information that Alzheimer's disease is best treated by a combination of drug and psychiatric therapies. But common knowledge extends beyond these very general types of information to more specific information within a field of study. In medical studies, for example, it is a widely known fact that Prozac is the trade name for fluoxetine hydrochloride; in education, a commonly acknowledged interpretation is that standardized tests do not uniformly produce success. Documenting these facts, beliefs, and interpretations in a paper would be unnecessary because they are commonly known in their areas of study, even though you might have discovered them for the first time.

When you are researching an unfamiliar subject, distinguishing common knowledge that does not require documentation from special knowledge that does require documentation is sometimes difficult. The following guidelines may help.

What constitutes common knowledge

- *Historical facts* (names, dates, and general interpretations) that appear in many general reference books. For example, Sigmund Freud's most influential work, *The Interpretation of Dreams,* was published in 1899.

- *General observations and opinions* that are shared by many people. For example, it is a general observation that children learn by actively doing, rather than passively listening, and it is a commonly held opinion that reading, writing, and arithmetic are the basic skills that should be learned by an elementary school child.

- *Unacknowledged information* that appears in multiple sources. For example, it is common knowledge that the earth's population is roughly 6 billion people and that an *IQ* is a gauge of intelligence determined by a person's knowledge in relation to his or her age.

If a piece of information does not meet these guidelines or if you are uncertain about whether it is common knowledge, always document the material.

SPECIAL QUALITIES OF SOURCE MATERIALS

A more difficult problem than identifying common knowledge involves using an author's words and ideas improperly. Improper use often results from careless summarizing and paraphrasing. To use source materials without plagiarizing, learn to recognize their distinctive qualities.

Special qualities of sources

- *Distinctive prose style:* The author's choices of words, phrases, and sentence patterns
- *Original facts:* The result of the author's personal research
- *Personal interpretations of information:* The author's individual evaluation of his or her information
- *Original ideas:* Those ideas that are unique to the particular author

As you work with sources, be aware of these distinguishing qualities and make certain that you do not appropriate the prose (word choices and sentence structures), original research, interpretations, or ideas of others without giving proper credit.

Consider, for example, the following paragraphs from Joyce Appleby, Lynn Hunt, and Margaret Jacob's *Telling the Truth About History* (New York: Norton, 1994):

> Interest in this new research in social history can be partly explained by the personal backgrounds of the cohort of historians who undertook the task of writing history from the bottom up. They entered higher education with the post-*Sputnik* expansion of the 1950s and 1960s, when the number of new Ph.D.s in history nearly quadrupled. Since many of them were children and grandchildren of immigrants, they had a personal

incentive for turning the writing of their dissertations into a movement of memory recovery. Others were black or female and similarly prompted to find ways to make the historically inarticulate speak. While the number of male Ph.D.s in history ebbed and flowed with the vicissitudes of the job market, the number of new female Ph.D.s in history steadily increased from 11 percent (29) in 1950 to 13 percent (137) in 1970 and finally to 37 percent (192) in 1989.

Although ethnicity is harder to locate in the records, the GI Bill was clearly effective in bringing the children of working-class families into the middle-class educational mainstream. This was the thin end of a democratizing wedge prying open higher education in the United States. Never before had so many people in any society earned so many higher degrees. Important as their numbers were, the change in perspective these academics brought to their disciplines has made the qualitative changes even more impressive. Suddenly graduate students with strange, unpronounceable surnames, with Brooklyn accents and different skin colors, appeared in the venerable ivy-colored buildings that epitomized elite schooling.

Now look at the following examples of faulty and acceptable summaries and paraphrases, noting in the faulty samples that questionable phrases are underlined.

Faulty summary: plagiarism likely

Appleby, Hunt, Jacob   historians' backgrounds

-- A historian's focus is <u>partially explained</u> by his or her <u>personal background.</u>

-- Because of their experiences, <u>they have a personal incentive</u> for looking at history in new ways.

-- Large numbers were important, but the change in viewpoint <u>made the qualitative changes even more impressive.</u>

pp. 146–147

Acceptable summary: plagiarism unlikely

Appleby, Hunt, Jacob   historians' background

-- A historian's focus and interpretations are personal.

-- For personal reasons, not always stated, people examine the facts of history from different perspectives.

-- Large numbers were important, but the change in viewpoint "made the qualitative changes even more impressive."

            pp. 146–147

Faulty paraphrase: plagiarism likely

Appleby, Hunt, Jacob   the GI Bill

-- <u>Even though ethnic background is not easily found</u> in the statistics, the GI Bill consistently helped students from <u>low-income families enter the middle-class educational system</u>. This was how <u>democracy started forcing open college education in America</u>.

            pp. 146–147

Acceptable paraphrase: plagiarism unlikely

Appleby, Hunt, Jacob   the GI Bill

-- Because of the GI Bill, even poor people could attend college. For the first time, education was accessible to everyone, which is truly democracy in action. The GI Bill was "the thin end of a democratizing wedge prying open higher education."

            pp. 146–147

1h Planning

After gathering information, organizing the research paper is an exciting stage because you are ready to bring ideas together in a clear and logical form.

REVIEWING NOTES

Begin by rereading the assignment sheet to re-examine the principles guiding your work. Then review your notes. Although it may be time-consuming, rereading all of your notes allows you to see the range of materials and connections among ideas.

THESIS STATEMENT OR STATED OBJECTIVE

After rereading your notes, revise the thesis statement or objective so that it accurately represents the paper you plan to write. Is the topic clear? Does it express your current (more informed) view? Does it contain appropriate qualifications and limitations? Is it worded effectively?

AN INFORMAL OUTLINE

An informal outline is a structural plan prepared for your own use. Arrange information in logical ways using numbers, arrows, dashes, dots, and other convenient symbols to indicate the order for presentation and the relative importance of ideas.

Using the major headings from the informal outline, sort your notes. If a note fits into more than one group, place it in the most appropriate group and place a cross-reference note (for example, "See Parker quotation, p. 219—in *Childhood*") in each of the other appropriate groups.

A FORMAL OUTLINE

If you choose to develop a formal outline, adhere to the following conventions to establish divisions within the outline:

- *Major topics.* Use upper-case roman numerals *(I, II, III)* to indicate major topics.
- *Subdivisions.* Use upper-case letters *(A, B, C)* to indicate subdivisions of the major topics.

- *Clarifications.* Use arabic numerals *(1, 2, 3)* to indicate clarifications of subdivisions—usually examples, supporting facts, and so on.
- *Details.* Use lower-case letters *(a, b, c)* to indicate details used to describe the examples.

In addition, observe the following conventions:

- Use parallel form throughout. Use words and phrases to develop a topic outline or use full sentences to develop a sentence outline.
- Include only one idea in each entry. Subdivide entries that contain two or more ideas.
- Include at least two entries at each sublevel.
- Indent headings of the same level the same number of spaces from the margin.

1i Writing Strategies

Because incorporating research materials and using in-text documentation extend the time it takes to write a paper, allow yourself ample time to complete the draft of your paper. Consider both the general and special circumstances that affect the process of writing and revising any paper, as well as those issues that relate specifically to writing and revising a research paper.

GENERAL STRATEGIES FOR DRAFTING A PAPER

Because the research paper is in many ways like all other papers, keep these general writing strategies in mind:

- *Gather materials.* Collect planning materials and writing supplies before you begin writing. Working consistently in the same location is also helpful because all materials are there when you wish to write.
- *Work from an outline.* Following an outline, develop paragraphs and sections; write troublesome sections late in the process.
- *Keep the paper's purpose in mind.* Arrange and develop only those ideas that your outline indicates are important.

- *Develop the paper "promised" by the thesis, hypothesis, or stated objective.* Incorporate only those ideas and information that support your thesis, hypothesis, or stated objective.

- *Attend to technical matters later.* Concentrate on getting your ideas down on paper; you can revise the paper later to correct any technical errors.

- *Rethink troublesome sections.* When sections are difficult to write, reconsider their importance or means of development. Revise the outline if necessary.

- *Reread as you write.* Reread early sections as you write in order to maintain a consistent tone and style of development.

- *Write alternative sections.* Write several versions of troublesome sections and then choose the best one.

- *Take periodic breaks.* Get away from your work for short periods so that you can maintain a fresh perspective and attain objectivity.

STRATEGIES FOR DRAFTING A RESEARCH PAPER

Because the research paper has its own peculiarities and demands, keep these special strategies in mind:

- *Allow ample time.* Give yourself plenty of time to write a research paper; its length and complexity will affect the speed at which you work.

- *Think about sections, not paragraphs.* Think of the paper in terms of sections, not paragraphs. Large sections will probably contain several paragraphs.

- *Use transitions.* Although headings will divide your work into logical segments, use well-chosen transitional words to signal major shifts between elements of the paper.

- *Attend to technical language.* Define technical terms carefully to clarify ideas.

- *Incorporate notes smoothly.* Use research materials to support and illustrate—not dominate—your discussion.

- *Document carefully.* Use in-text citations (parenthetical notes) to acknowledge the sources of your ideas and information. (See chapter 4, "Preparing the Reference List and In-Text Citations.")

QUESTIONS FOR REVISING CONTENT

Examine the paper's content for clarity, coherence, and completeness. Consider these issues:

- *Title, introduction, headings, conclusion.*   Are your title, introduction, headings, and conclusion well-matched to the tone and purpose of the paper?
- *Thesis (hypothesis) and development.*   Does the thesis accurately represent your current view on the topic, and does the paper develop that idea?
- *Support for thesis.*   Do research materials effectively support the paper's thesis? Have you eliminated material (details, sentences, even paragraphs) that does not directly support your thesis?
- *Organization.*   Does your organizational pattern present your ideas logically and effectively?
- *Use of materials.*   Have you incorporated a range of materials to develop your ideas in a varied, interesting, and complete way?
- *Balance among sections.*   Are the sections of the paper balanced in length and emphasis?
- *Balance among sources.*   Have you used a variety of sources to support your ideas?
- *Transitions.*   Do transitions connect sections of the paper in a coherent way?

QUESTIONS FOR REVISING STYLE

Achieving coherent, balanced, well-developed content is one aspect of revision. Another consideration is achieving a clear and compelling presentation of that content. Refine the paper's style, keeping these issues in mind:

- *Tone.*   Is the tone suited to the topic and presentation?
- *Sentences.*   Are the sentences varied in both length and type? Have you written active, rather than passive, sentences?
- *Diction.*   Are the word choices vivid, accurate, and suitable?
- *Introduction of research materials.*   Have you introduced research materials (facts, summaries, paraphrases, and quotations) with variety and clarity?

QUESTIONS FOR REVISING TECHNICAL MATTERS

Technical revision focuses on grammar, punctuation, mechanics, spelling, and manuscript form. After revising content and style, consider technical revisions to make the presentation correct and precise, giving particular attention to issues related to documentation:

• *Grammar.* Are your sentences complete? Do nouns agree with pronouns, and subjects with verbs? Have you worked to avoid errors that you commonly make?

• *Punctuation and mechanics.* Have you double-checked your punctuation? Have you spell-checked the paper? Have you used quotation marks and italics correctly?

• *Quotations.* Are quotations presented correctly, depending on their length or emphasis?

• *In-text citations.* Are in-text citations (parenthetical notes) placed appropriately and punctuated correctly?

• *Reference list.* Have you listed only the sources actually used in the paper? Is your list alphabetized correctly? Is each entry complete and correct?

• *Manuscript guidelines.* Are margins, line spacing, and paging correct? Does the paper include all necessary elements?

Preparing APA Manuscripts

APA style guidelines for manuscript preparation ensure that manuscripts follow uniform standards and, as a result, present the elements of papers in a generally understood way.

2a Parts of the Manuscript

A manuscript for an APA paper can contain as many as ten separate parts: the title page, abstract, paper, reference list, appendixes, author's note, footnotes, tables, figure captions, and figures. Not all papers have all of these features, but when they do, they are arranged in this order.

The first part of this chapter addresses the specific requirements for preparing each element of an APA paper. The last part of the chapter addresses general manuscript guidelines.

TITLE PAGE

A manuscript prepared in APA style begins with a separate title page (see page 110 for a sample), composed of the following elements:

- *Page information.* On the first line of the title page, provide a page header (see page 111 for a sample); for full instructions to creating a page header, see "Paging (Page Header)" on page 35. The title page is page 1 of the manuscript.

- *Running head.* The first page-specific element is the running head, a short version of the paper's title. Two spaces below the page header, at the left margin, type *Running head* (not italicized, but followed by a colon) and an abbreviated version of the paper's title; it can contain no more than fifty characters (letters, numbers, symbols, punctuation, and spaces). The running head is typed in all capital letters, and a shortened version is used in the page header.

- *Title.* Center the title and capitalize all major words. A good title is descriptive, clarifying both the topic and the perspective of the paper; when possible, the

Parts of an APA Paper

- *Title page.* The opening page highlights the title of the paper, provides identifying information about the author, and incorporates information to label the pages of the paper.

- *Abstract.* This detailed paragraph presents a brief overview of the paper, emphasizing key ideas and briefly explaining research procedures.

- *Paper.* An informative or persuasive paper contains an introduction, body, and conclusion; it is frequently divided using headings that describe the main elements of the discussion. A research study contains an introduction of the problem, an explanation of methodology, a summary of results, and a discussion of the implications of the study.

- *Reference list.* The alphabetically arranged reference list provides publishing information about the sources used in the paper.

- *Appendixes.* Appendixes provide supplementary information that supports the ideas in the paper but that is awkward to include in the paper itself.

- *Author's note.* The note identifies the affiliation of the author, acknowledges financial support, recognizes the contributions of other people, and explains how to contact the author. The author may also disclose any special circumstances related to the writing of the paper.

- *Footnotes.* Content footnotes include clarifying discussions and explanations that might disrupt the flow of the paper. The numbered footnotes that appear on the footnote page correspond to numbers placed within the text of the paper.

- *Tables.* Numbered tables include technical data in easily interpreted and comparable forms. References within the paper correspond to tables that appear on separate pages near the end of the manuscript.

- *Figure captions.* The printed captions that accompany figures appear in this separately prepared list. Labels that include figure numbers ensure that the correct caption is used with each figure.

> - *Figures.*   Visual images to support ideas in a paper (drawings, graphs, photographs, maps, and so on) appear as numbered figures. References within the paper correspond to figures that appear on separate pages at the end of the manuscript.

title should also create interest through effective wording. APA recommends that titles be fewer than twelve words long (a title of this length generally fits on a single line). If the title must be longer than one line to be clear, divide it logically and center both lines.

- *Author's name.*   Two lines below the title, include your name (centered and capitalized normally). On the line below your name, list your affiliation; you can use your school's name, the title of the course for which you have written the paper, or the city and state in which you live.
- *Centered information.*   After typing the title, your name, and other identifying information, center this information on the page vertically (making sure that at least one line of the title appears in the top half of the page). This key information, as a result, is centered from top to bottom and from left to right.

ABSTRACT

The abstract follows the title page (it is page 2 of the manuscript) and provides a brief description of the major ideas in the paper (see page 110 for a sample). Because it must summarize the full range of ideas and information in the paper, it is generally written after the manuscript is complete. It must adhere to the following guidelines:

- *Heading.*   Two lines below the page header, type *Abstract,* centered but not italicized. Two lines below it, begin the paragraph.
- *Format.*   The abstract is a single, unindented, double-spaced paragraph.
- *Length.*   The abstract can be no more than 120 words.

- *Concision.* To save space in the abstract, use standard abbreviations (*AMA,* rather than *American Medical Association*); use digits for all numbers, except those that begin sentences; and use active, rather than passive, sentences.
- *Content.* In the opening sentence, describe the topic or problem addressed in the paper. Use the remaining words in the paragraph to clarify methodology (for a research study), to identify major ideas, and to explain results or conclusions. If a paper is lengthy and multi-faceted, describe only the most important elements.

THE TEXT

The text of the paper begins on the third page of the manuscript (see pages 111–116 for sample pages). The page header, as always, appears on the top line. Two spaces below, center the title, with all important words capitalized. Two spaces below the title, the paper begins. The organization of the body of the paper depends on its focus.

An Argumentative Paper or Review

- *Introduction.* In this unlabeled section, define, describe, or clarify the topic (problem); place it in its historical or scholarly context. Present a thesis (a statement of your topic and opinion).

- *Body.* Examine the facets of the topic (problem) by reviewing current research: evaluate the positions held by others; analyze current data; assess the interpretations of others; synthesize the information and ideas found in other people's work. Use headings and subheadings throughout this section to direct readers through your argument.

- *Conclusion.* Summarize key points, draw connections among important ideas, and reiterate your thesis.

- *Reference list.* This labeled section provides a list of sources cited in the paper (see chapter 4).

- *Additional materials.* As appropriate, include the following labeled sections: appendixes, author's note, footnotes, tables, figure captions, and figures.

A Research Study

- *Introduction.*   In this unlabeled section, describe the problem, state your hypothesis, and describe your research methodology. Consider the importance of the problem, the ways in which the study addresses the problem, and the implications of previous scholarly research.

- *Literature review.*   This labeled section provides a summary of scholarship on the paper's topic. It should present a historical or contextual discussion of what scholars have written, acknowledging alternative perspectives and differing interpretations.

- *Method.*   This labeled section should be divided into labeled subsections that describe participants in the study (and procedures for selecting them), materials used (ranging from standard equipment to custom materials), and procedures (the step-by-step process for conducting the research).

- *Results.*   This labeled section summarizes the gathered information. It should be further subdivided into labeled subsections that analyze information that is illustrated by tables, figures, and other statistical material.

- *Discussion.*   This labeled section should open with an assertion about the correlation of your data with your original hypothesis. The remaining discussion can address how your findings relate to the work of others, what qualifications are necessary, what the value of alternative interpretations is, or what conclusions you have reached. End the discussion by commenting on the significance of your research results.

- *Reference list.*   This labeled section provides a list of sources cited in the paper (see chapter 4).

- *Additional materials.*   As appropriate, include the following labeled sections: appendixes, author's note, footnotes, tables, figure captions, and figures.

REFERENCE LIST

The reference list, which continues the paging of the entire manuscript, provides publishing information for all sources used in the paper (see page 117 for samples). Chapter 4 provides a comprehensive discussion of the information required in reference-list entries and the format for presenting the information. Chapters 5–8 provide explanations of fifty-nine kinds of sources, with samples for preparing reference-list entries for periodicals, books and other print materials, audiovisual sources, and electronic sources (with corresponding in-text citations).

APPENDIXES

One or more appendixes follow the reference list and continue the page numbering of the entire manuscript. Each appendix should adhere to the following guidelines:

- *Heading.* Two lines below the page header, type *Appendix,* centered but not italicized. If more than one appendix is included, label each one with a letter *(Appendix A, Appendix B).*
- *Appendix title.* Two lines below the heading, type the title of the appendix, centered, with all major words capitalized.
- *Text.* Begin the text two lines below the appendix title; appended material is double-spaced.
- *Paging.* An appendix begins on a new page. If a paper includes more than one appendix, each one starts on a new page.

AUTHOR'S NOTE

An author's note, which begins on a new page, provides brief clarifying information about the author and includes the following elements:

- *Heading.* Two lines below the page header, type *Author Note,* centered but not italicized.
- *Text.* Begin the text two lines below the label. Use separate, indented paragraphs for each of these elements: (1) the author's name and affiliation, (2) acknowledgments, and (3) the author's contact information.
- *Paging.* An author's note begins on a new page.

FOOTNOTES

Content footnotes allow writers to provide additional discussion or clarification that—although important— might disrupt the flow of a paper.

Footnotes appear on a new page and follow these guidelines for placement and presentation:

- *Heading.* Two lines below the page header, type *Footnotes,* centered but not italicized.

- *Order of notes.* Footnotes appear on the footnote page in the order in which references appear in the paper. Double-check the numbering.

- *Format.* Footnotes are typed in paragraph style, with the first line indented and subsequent lines aligned at the left margin. "Tab" once (for a five-space indention), insert the appropriate superscript number, and type the footnote. No space separates the note number from the first letter of the first word of the footnote.

- *Paging.* Footnotes continue the paging of the manuscript. Multiple footnotes may appear on the same page, with no additional space separating the notes.

Placing Note Numbers in the Paper

- *In-text notes.* Footnotes are numbered sequentially throughout a paper.

- *Placement of in-text note numbers.* In the text of the paper, refer to a content note by using a superscript number (a number placed above the line, like this[1]) without additional space. Word-processing programs allow you to achieve this result by using the "font" feature.

- *Punctuation and note numbers.* Note numbers follow all punctuation marks, except dashes and parentheses. A note number precedes the dash[2]— without additional space. A note number may appear within parentheses (when it refers only to materials with the parentheses[3]). If the note refers to the entire sentence, however, it follows the parentheses (as in this sample).[4]

TABLES

Because tables present labeled information in columns (vertical separations) and rows (horizontal separations) for easy interpretation or comparison, they are helpful additions to papers that use technical data (see page 126 for a sample). Within the paper, a reference (for example, *see Table 1, as illustrated in Table 2*) directs readers to tables using numerals (which correspond to tables presented near the end of the manuscript). Tables are prepared on separate pages and are presented according to these principles:

- *Table identification.* Two spaces below the page header (flush with the left margin), type *Table* and the table's arabic numeral *(Table 3, Table 4)*, not italicized.

- *Title of the table.* Two spaces below the table heading, also flush left, type the title of the table, capitalizing all important words and placing the entire title in italics. One line below, insert a horizontal ruled line; use the graphics or "Insert" feature of your word-processing program to create this element.

- *Column headings.* Capitalize only the first word of column headings and center the column heading over the information in each column. One line below the column headings, insert a horizontal ruled line.

- *Spacing.* Tables are double-spaced, no matter how long they are. Columns must be separated by at least three spaces for visual clarity.

- *Repeated information.* If information from a table extends beyond one page, repeat the column headings.

- *Table notes (general).* If you need to provide an explanation of an entire table, provide a general note. One line below the body of the table, insert a horizontal ruled line. Two spaces below this line, type *Note* (italicized and flush with the left margin), followed by a period; after one space, type the text of your note, which remains flush left if it extends beyond one line.

- *Table notes (specific).* If you need to provide an explanation of a specific element within a table, provide a specific note. (Within the table, insert a superscript lowercase letter—like this[a]—following the element.) One line below the body of the table, insert a horizontal ruled line. Two spaces below this line and flush with the left margin, insert the corresponding superscript lowercase letter, followed by the explanation.

- *Paging.*　Each table must begin on a new page.

FIGURE CAPTIONS

Placed on a separate manuscript page, a list of figure captions corresponds to the separate figures that appear on subsequent manuscript pages (see page 127 for a sample). Follow these guidelines:

- *Heading.*　Two lines below the page header, type *Figure Captions,* centered but not italicized.
- *Figure identification.*　Two lines below the label, flush left, type the word *Figure,* the number of the figure, and a period. All of these elements are italicized.
- *Figure caption.*　One space after the figure identification, type the caption, capitalizing only the first word and any proper nouns or proper adjectives. Place a period at the end of the caption, whether it is a sentence or a phrase. The caption is not italicized.
- *Spacing and indention.*　Figure captions are double-spaced. If a caption extends beyond one line, it continues flush left.
- *Paging.*　Multiple figure captions may appear on the same page, with no additional space separating the captions.

FIGURES

Figures are visual elements—drawings, graphs, photographs, maps, and so on—that cannot be reproduced by traditional typing (see page 127 for a sample). Each figure is numbered as it is used in the paper; original figures then appear on separate pages at the end of the manuscript, following these guidelines:

- *Heading.*　Two lines below the page header, type *Figure* with an arabic numeral, not italicized.
- *Figure.*　Present the highest-quality figure possible, with sharp contrast in photographs, distinct shading in bar graphs, and clear lettering in line graphs. Remember, also, that figures must be scaled to fit appropriately on the page.

- *Fonts.* Printed text that is part of a figure—labels, for example—should use a sans serif font such as **Helvetica.** The minimum acceptable font size is 8 points, with 14 points being the maximum.
- *Paging.* Each figure must be presented on a new page.

Special Concerns for Figures

- *Value of the figure.* Consider whether the figure presents information more effectively than would a textual discussion or a table. Because figures are more difficult to prepare than print-based elements, make sure that your time is well spent in creating one.

- *Computer-generated figures.* Today's word-processing programs are capable of creating a wide range of figures, including bar graphs, line graphs, and pie charts. Allow sufficient time to learn to use these computer features.

- *Visual clutter.* Include only figures that highlight important elements of your discussion. To achieve this goal, eliminate all extraneous detail in graphs, charts, and drawings and crop (trim) photographs and maps to focus visual attention on key features, not superficial or unrelated elements.

- *Visual clarity.* To ensure that figures achieve maximum impact, make sure that the print quality of graphs and charts is high (best achieved by laser printing). Furthermore, make sure that bar charts, photographs, and maps are sharply focused and have clear contrast in their tones.

2b General Manuscript Guidelines

In preparing a paper in APA style, writers must conform to a variety of principles, each of which is described in the following sections.

PAPER

Use heavy-weight, white bond, 8½" × 11" paper. Avoid onionskin and erasable paper; neither holds up well under review or grading. If you must work on erasable paper, submit a high-quality photocopy on good-quality paper.

FONT SELECTION

Fonts—designed versions of letters, numbers, and characters—appear in different sizes, referred to as *points*. APA encourages the use of serif fonts (those with cross marks on individual letters) for the text of the paper; **Times Roman** and `Courier` are preferred. Sans serif fonts (those without cross marks) such as **Arial** or **Century Gothic** should be used to label figures and illustrations. Font sizes for all elements of the paper except for figures should be 12 points, the default size in most word-processing programs.

Use italics *(slanted type)*, not underlining, in all parts of your paper. Also take advantage of your word processor's capabilities to insert accents, diacritical marks, and symbols directly in your paper, rather than adding them by hand.

LINE SPACING

Double-space everything: the elements of the title page, abstract, paper, reference list, and any supplementary material. For visual clarity, you may triple- or quadruple-space between elements of the paper; however, never use less than double-spacing.

MARGINS AND INDENTIONS

Leave one-inch margins at the left, right, top, and bottom of each page. If the "default" margins for your word-processing program are not one inch, reset them. Do not justify the right margin (that is, create a straight text edge on the right); instead, use left justification, which aligns the text on the left but leaves the right margin irregular (ragged). Do not hyphenate words at the ends of lines.

Indent paragraphs five spaces using the "Tab" feature. Use the "Indent" feature (which establishes a continuous five-space indention) for long quotations and for second and subsequent lines in entries in the reference list.

PAGING (PAGE HEADER)

The page header consists of a brief version of the paper's running head (usually the first two or three words), followed by five spaces and then a page number (without page abbreviation). Starting with the title page, it appears in the upper-right corner of each manuscript page. This information must be at least one-half inch from the top of the page; two spaces below, the text begins (see page 121 for a sample).

Use the "Header" feature of your word-processing program to insert page information throughout the manuscript. Set the header at the beginning of the document, move the cursor flush with the right margin, and then type a brief version of the running head, five spaces, and the code to insert page numbers automatically.

HEADINGS FOR SECTIONS

Use headings to divide and subdivide the paper into logical, and sometimes sequential, sections. APA establishes five potential levels of division for manuscripts, while acknowledging that most writing does not require the use of all five:

- *Level-5 headings* are centered, with all letters capitalized.
- *Level-1 headings* are centered, with all major words capitalized.
- *Level-2 headings* are centered, with all major words capitalized and italicized.
- *Level-3 headings* are flush left, with all major words capitalized and italicized.
- *Level-4 headings* are indented, with only the first word capitalized. They are italicized and followed by a period. After one space, the text continues on the same line.

One level of division

> Level-1 Heading

Two levels of division

> Level-1 Heading
> *Level-3 Heading*

Three levels of division

Level-1 Heading
Level-3 Heading
Level-4 heading.

Four levels of division

Level-1 Heading
Level-2 Heading
Level-3 Heading
Level-4 heading.

Five levels of division

LEVEL-5 HEADING
Level-1 Heading
Level-2 Heading
Level-3 Heading
Level-4 heading.

When new headings are required, do not begin new pages. Simply continue two lines below the heading.

SUBMITTING THE PAPER

Submit manuscripts according to your instructor's guidelines. If you receive no specific guidelines, secure the pages with a paper clip in the upper-left corner and place them in a manila envelope with your name and course information typed or written on the outside. Always keep a photocopy—or another printed copy—of the paper.

Be aware that instructors may ask for a computer file version of the paper. In that case, submit a copy of the final paper on a separate disk, clearly labeled with your name and course information. Keep a disk version for yourself as well.

Generally, APA style follows conventions that need little explanation (for example, periods follow sentences that make statements, and question marks follow sentences that pose questions). However, in some situations, agreement about editorial issues is not universal (Should commas separate *all* elements of listed items? Are prepositions in titles capitalized?). In such special circumstances, follow the APA guidelines in this chapter to ensure that your manuscript meets expectations.

3a Punctuation and Mechanics

PERIODS

Periods most often serve as end punctuation (after sentences), but they are also used with abbreviations and in other specialized contexts.

Uses of periods	Examples
End of a complete sentence	A period is followed by one space.
Initials with an author's name	C. S. Lewis
Reference-list abbreviations	Ed., Vol. 6, pp. 34–38, Rev. ed.
After figure captions	*Figure 3.* Student use of computers.
Latin abbreviations	i.e., e.g., vs., p.m.
U.S. when used as an adjective	U.S. government, U.S. economy
Abbreviation for inch	in. (distinct from the preposition *in*)
Decimal points in fractions	0.76 cm, 2.45 ml, 33.5 lb

COMMAS

Commas are internal forms of punctuation, most often used to separate elements within sentences. However, they also serve a few other purposes.

Uses of commas	Examples
Three or more items in a series	men, women, and children
Set off nonessential information	The room, which was well lighted, was on the south corridor.
Clauses of a compound sentence	The first presentation was a failure, but the second one was a success.
Years with exact dates	May 25, 2001, the experiment began. *But* May 2001 the experiment began.
Years in in-text citations	(Armstrong, 2002); (Kindervader, 2000, observed . . .)
Numbers of 1,000 or larger (every three numbers)	11,205 students, 1,934 books [see "Number Style," page 49, for exceptions]

SEMICOLONS

In APA style, semicolons serve two purposes, one related to compound sentences and one related to elements in a series. (See box, page 40.)

COLONS

Colons serve three distinct purposes in APA style. A complete sentence must precede the colon, and if the explanatory material that follows a colon is a complete sentence, the first word is capitalized.

Uses of semicolons	Examples
Join clauses of a compound sentence when no coordinating conjunction is used	Males responded positively; females responded less positively.
Separate elements in a series when the elements contain commas	The test groups were from Fresno, California; St. Louis, Missouri; and Raleigh, North Carolina.

Uses of colons	Examples
Introduce a phrase or clause that serves as an explanation or illustration	Two words triggered the strongest reactions: *preferential* and *special.* (Phrase) The results are quickly summarized: The experiment was a failure. (Clause)
Separate elements in a ratio	The correlation was 3:10.
Separate the place of publication and publisher in a reference-list entry	Perrin, R. (2005). *Handbook for college research* (3rd ed.). Boston: Houghton.

DASHES

Formed by typing two hyphens with no spaces before and after, dashes serve a few selected purposes; however, they should be used selectively in academic writing. Also note that if a title contains a dash, the word that follows a dash is capitalized. (See box, page 41.)

QUOTATION MARKS

Quotation marks are used within the body of a paper to identify titles of some works, to indicate a quotation containing fewer than forty words, and to highlight words

Uses of dashes	Examples
Indicate a break in the thought of the sentence	The national heritage of participants--they identified themselves--proved less important than we anticipated.
Insert a series of elements that contain commas	Universities in two small cities--Terre Haute, Indiana, and Bloomington, Illinois--offer similar degree programs in psychology.

Uses of quotation marks	Examples
Titles of chapters, articles, songs, subsites of Web sites, and so on (used in the text only; reference-list entries *do not* use quotation marks)	"The High-Risk Child" (chapter), "Grant Writing vs. Grant Getting" (article), "My Vietnam" (song), "Alderian Web Links" (subsite)
Quoted material (written or spoken) of fewer than forty words when used word for word	Duncan (2002) asserted, "Normative behavior is difficult to define because community standards come into play" (p. 233).
Words used counter to their intended meaning (irony, slang, or coined usage)	Her "abnormal" behavior was, in fact, quite normal.

used in special ways. Note especially that quotation marks are not used in reference-list entries and that quotations of more than forty words are indented and use no quotation marks. (See pages 68–71 for additional information on quoted material.)

PARENTHESES

Parentheses are used—always in pairs—to separate information and elements from the rest of the sentence.

Uses of parentheses	Examples
Set off clarifying information	We provided parents with four samples (see Figures 1–4).
Set off parenthetical references within the text; they must correspond to entries in the reference list.	First-time offenders are more likely to respond to group therapy sessions than are repeat offenders (Gillum & Sparks, 2000).
Set off page references that follow direct quotations	Rodriguez (2002) noted, "Self-concept is an intangible quality among immigrant children" (p. 34).
Introduce an abbreviation to be used in place of a full name in subsequent sections of a paper	Conference on College Composition and Communication (CCCC) hosts its annual conference in the spring. Graduate students attend CCCC in ever-increasing numbers.
Set off numbers or letters that indicate divisions or sequences	The test included sections on (1) vocabulary, (2) reading comprehension, (3) inferences, and (4) error identification.

BRACKETS

Brackets are used within parentheses or quotation marks to provide clarifying information. Use brackets sparingly because they can become distracting in academic writing.

Uses of brackets	Examples
Parenthetical information already in parentheses	(See Figure 4 [Percentages of students with learning disabilities] for more detailed information.)
Clarifying information in a quotation	Thompson (2001) observed, "When [students] work in groups, they are more comfortable and perform better" (p. 11).

SLASHES

Slashes serve very specialized functions, often related to the presentation of compounds, comparisons, and correlations.

Uses of slashes	Examples
Hyphenated compounds in alternatives	first-day/second-day experiences
Fractions (numerator/denominator)	3/4, X + Y/Z
Represent *per* in units with numerical value	0.7 ml/L
Indicate phonemes in English	/b/
Separate dual publication dates	Palmer (1930/1968)

CAPITALIZATION

APA patterns for capitalization are distinct. The universally accepted practice of capitalizing the first word of sentences and capitalizing proper or specific names causes few problems; however, APA uses two patterns of capitalization for titles: one pattern for titles in the text and one pattern for those in the reference list.

Uses of capitalization	Examples
Proper nouns and proper adjectives	Jean Piaget, Robert Coles, Chinese students, Elizabethan drama
Specific departments (and academic units) in universities and specific courses	Department of Psychology, Indiana State University, Criminology 235
Trade and brand names	Prozac, Xerox, WordPerfect 9.0
Specific titles for parts of books	"The Middle-Child Syndrome" (*but* chapter 4)
Nouns used with numbers or letters in describing sequenced methods or examples	Day 4, Experiment 6, Table 1, Figure 3A
Formal titles of tests	Scholastic Aptitude Test
Table titles: Capitalize all important words.	*Grade Ranges of First-Year Students* (table title)
First word of a sentence following a colon	One challenge could not be met: The cost for administering the test was too great.

Capitalization of Titles

APA follows two distinct patterns for the capitalization of titles: one within the text of a paper and one in the reference list and other supporting pages.

- *In-text capitalization.* In the text of a paper—both in your prose and in in-text citations (parenthetical notes)—the first words of titles and subtitles and all major words are capitalized, whether they are periodicals, books, audiovisual sources, or electronic sources. However, conjunctions and prepositions of fewer than four letters (*or, but, and, as, for, to*) are not capitalized, nor are articles (*a, an, the*).

Special cases—No capitalization	Examples
Hyphenated compound: second word	D. P. Becker. (1996). *Short-term Memory Loss.*
Figure captions: Capitalize only the first word.	*Figure 1.* Percentages of international students by country of origin
General references to departments and courses	a number of departments of sociology, a speech pathology course
Generic or scientific names of drugs or ingredients	fluoxetine hydrochloride (*but* Prozac)
General names of laws or theories	the empirical law of effect
Standard parts of books or tables	chapter 16, column 2, row 6
General titles of tests	an achievement test

Book

In *The Mismeasure of Man,* Gould (1981) provides useful insights into the ethical and unethical uses to which intelligence tests can be put.

Periodical

Mokhtari and Reichard (2002), in their *Journal of Educational Psychology* article "Assessing Students' Metacognitive Awareness of Reading Strategies," describe and analyze a new self-report instrument used to gauge students' procedures for reading school-related materials.

• *Reference-list (and other) capitalization.*　In the reference list, the titles of periodicals are capitalized according to the principles of in-text capitalization (see above). For titles of articles and all other sources (such as books or broadcasts), only the first words of titles and subtitles and proper nouns and proper adjectives are capitalized; all other words appear in lowercase letters.

Book

> Gould, S. J. (1981). *The mismeasure of man.* New York:
> Norton.

Periodical

> Mokhtari, K., & Reichard, C. A. Assessing students'
> metacognitive awareness of reading strategies.
> *Journal of Educational Psychology, 94,* 249–259.

To present descriptive titles of supporting materials such as tables, figures, and figure captions, capitalize only the first words of titles and subtitles and proper nouns and proper adjectives.

A special note: On the title page, the running head appears in all capital letters. In the page header, however, only the first letters of major words are capitalized.

ITALICS

APA recommends the use of italics (slanted fonts, as in *this example*), rather than underlining, in computer-generated manuscripts.

Uses of italics	Examples
Titles of full-length works: periodicals, books, films, albums, Web sites, and so on	*Journal of Cognitive Psychology* (journal), *Wordplay and Language Learning* (book), *A Beautiful Mind* (film), *The Lillywhite Sessions* (album), *The Victorian Web* (Web site)
Genus, species, or varieties	*Pan troglodytes verus* (common chimpanzee)
New terms (introduced and defined)	The term *Nisei,* meaning second-generation Japanese Americans
Words, letters, or phrases used as words, letters, or phrases	Different impressions are created by the words *small, diminutive, minute,* and *tiny.*

Words that could be misread	*more* specific detail (meaning additional detail that is specific)
Letters used as symbols or algebraic variables	$IQ = \dfrac{MA \text{ (mental age)}}{CA \text{ (chronological age)}} \times 100$
Titles of tables	*Factors That Influence School Choice*
Volume numbers for periodicals (in reference-list entries)	*American Psychologist, 121;* *English Journal, 88*
Anchors for scales	Satisfaction ratings ranged from 1 *(very satisfied)* to 8 *(very dissatisfied)*.

NUMBER STYLE

In APA style, numerals are used more frequently than words, whether in written texts or supporting materials.

Uses of numerals	*Examples*
Numbers of 10 and larger	14 respondents, 26 chapters, 11th article
Numbers smaller than 10 when compared with numbers larger than 10	the 4th chapter of 20, 2 of 30 research subjects, 15 sources: 3 books, 10 articles, 1 interview, and 1 film
Numbers preceding units of measurement	6 in. mark, 300-mg capsule
Numbers used statistically or mathematically	7.5 of respondents, a ratio of 5:2, 9% of the sample, the 3rd percentile, multiplied by 3

(Continued)

Uses of numerals	Examples
Numbers that represent times	6 years, 5 months, 1 week, 3 hr, 15 min, 7:15 p.m.
Numbers that represent dates	April 1, 2001; November 9, 2002
Numbers that represent ages	4-year-olds, students who are 8 years old
Numbers for population size	1 million citizens
Numbers that refer to participants or subjects	7 participants, 4 rhesus monkeys
Numbers that refer to points or scores on a scale	scores of 6.5 on an 8-point scale
Numbers for exact sums of money	the cost of the test was $4.25, a $5 fee
Numbers used as numbers	a scale ranging from *1* to *5*
Numbers that indicate placement in a series	Exam 4, Figure 9
Numbers for parts of books	chapter 2, page 6
Numbers in a list of four or more numbers	The sample was composed of workgroups with 2, 4, 6, and 8 members.
Numbers in the abstract	All numbers appear in numeral form.

Cardinal and Ordinal Numbers

Cardinal numbers (one, two, three, and so on) indicate quantity; ordinal numbers (first, second, third, and so on) indicate order. The principles described in the preceding tables apply, whether the numbers are cardinal or ordinal.

Commas in Numbers

In most writing contexts, commas are used in numbers of 1,000 or larger. Place commas between groups of three digits, moving from the right. However, in the following seven situations, commas are not used.

Uses of words for numbers	*Examples*
Numbers smaller than 10 (see exceptions in the previous table)	two experimental models, three lists, one-topic discussion
Zero (when confusion is likely)	zero-percent increase
Numbers that begin sentences	Sixteen authors contributed to the collection. Thirteen observers approved.
Numbers that begin titles	"Twelve Common Errors in Research," *Seven-Point Scales: Values and Limitations*
Numbers that begin headings	Five common income groups (table heading)
Numbers in common fractions	two-thirds of teachers, a three-fourths reduction
Numbers in common names and phrases	the Seven Deadly Sins, the Ten Commandments, the Seven Wonders of the World

Numbers without commas	*Examples*
Page numbers	page 1287, pages 1002–1021, (p. 2349)
Degrees of temperature	2044 °F
Serial numbers	033776901
Binary digits	01100100
Numbers to the right of decimal points	2.09986
Designations of acoustical frequency	1000 Hz
Degrees of freedom	$F(31, 1000)$

Plurals of Numbers

Whether numbers are presented as numerals or words, form their plurals by adding only *s* or *es*. Do not use apostrophes to indicate plurality: 1960s, threes, 25s.

3b General Style

The way in which a manuscript is written affects the ways in which readers respond. A well-written paper communicates ideas efficiently and effectively, whereas a poorly written paper distracts readers from its central ideas.

Transitional Words and Phrases	
Relationship	*Examples*
Addition	also, and, besides, equally, further, furthermore, in addition, moreover, next, too
Similarity	also, likewise, moreover, similarly
Difference	but, however, in contrast, nevertheless, on the contrary, on the other hand, yet
Examples	for example, for instance, in fact, specifically, to illustrate
Restatements	finally, in brief, in conclusion, in other words, in short, in summary, on the whole, that is, therefore, to sum up
Results	accordingly, as a result, consequently, for this reason, so, therefore, thereupon, thus
Chronology	after, afterward, before, during, earlier, finally, first, immediately, in the meantime, later, meanwhile, next, second, simultaneously, soon, still, then, third, when, while
Location	above, below, beyond, farther, here, nearby, opposite, there, to the left, to the right, under

Consequently, take time to revise your writing to improve its presentation, especially considering a few key elements that improve the effectiveness of communication.

TRANSITIONS

Transitions—words or phrases that signal relationships among elements of a paper—facilitate readers' progress through a paper. Use transitions to create appropriate links within your work. (See box, page 50.)

VERB TENSE

Verbs are primary communicators in sentences, signaling action *(organize, summarize, present)* or indicating a state

Uses of verbs	*Examples*
Active voice (to clarify who is doing what)	Respondents completed the questionnaire in 15 minutes. (*Not:* The questionnaire was completed in 15 minutes by the respondents.)
Passive voice (to clarify who or what received the action, not the person or people responsible)	Traditional IQ tests were administered as part of the admissions process. (The use of the tests is emphasized, not the givers of the tests.)
Past tense (to place an action in the past or to describe previous research)	Bradshaw and Hines (2000) summarized their results in one incisive paragraph.
Present perfect tense (to describe an action that began in the past and continues to the present)	In the years since, researchers have incorporated Piaget's methods in a variety of studies of children.
Subjunctive mood (to describe a conditional situation or one contrary to fact)	If the sampling were larger, the results might be different.

of being *(seem, was)*. Well-chosen, specific verbs make writing direct and forceful. Moreover, tenses of verbs indicate chronology, clarifying the time relationships that you want to express.

In APA style, verbs are used in specific ways to signal ideas clearly. (See box, page 51.)

AGREEMENT

Agreement is the matching of words or word forms according to number (singular and plural) and gender (masculine, feminine, or neuter). Verbs take singular or plural forms depending on whether their subjects are singular or plural. Pronouns must match their antecedents (the words to which they refer) in both number and gender.

Subject–Verb Agreement

Special circumstances	*Examples*
Foreign words — *datum* (singular) versus *data* (plural), *phenomenon* (singular) versus *phenomena* (plural), and others: Choose the correct form.	The data suggest that our preconceptions were ill founded. (plural subject/plural verb) The phenomenon is unlikely to occur again. (singular subject/ singular verb)
Collective (or group) nouns: Consider whether members of the group act in unison (singular) or individually (plural).	The couple initiates the counseling sessions. (singular meaning to stress shared action) The couple meet separately with the counselor. (plural meaning to stress individual action)
Singular and plural subjects joined by *or* or *nor:* Match the verb to the nearer subject.	Neither the parents nor the therapist finds their meetings helpful. *Or:* Neither the therapist nor the parents find their meetings helpful.

Pronoun–Antecedent Agreement

Special circumstances	Examples
Agreement in number: Match the pronoun to its antecedent. (*Also see* "Biased Language," pages 56–58.)	A participant can secure his or her stipend from the controller's office. (singular) Participants can secure their stipends from the controller's office. (plural)
Agreement in gender: Match the pronoun to the antecedent. (*Also see* "Biased Language.")	Devon was the first student to complete his booklet. (masculine) The lab rat (subject 3) stopped eating its food during the experiment. (neuter)
Who and *whom:* Use *who* in a subject position; use *whom* in an object position.	Who is responsible for compiling the data? (subject: *He or she* is.) To whom should we address our inquiries? (object: Address it to *him or her.*)

PARALLELISM

Parallelism is the use of equivalent forms when words are used together: nouns, verbs of the same tense or form, and so on

Special circumstances	Examples
Elements in a series: Use matching forms.	Even young children are expected to add, to subtract, and to multiply. (parallel verb forms) Reading, writing, speaking, listening, and thinking compose the language arts. (parallel gerund/noun forms)

(Continued)

Special circumstances	Examples
Correlative conjunctions (*both/and, either/or, neither/nor, not only/but also):* Use matching forms of the words, phrases, and clauses that are linked.	The youngest child in a large family is either the most independent or the least independent of the siblings. (parallel phrases) We found not only that the experiment was too costly but also that it was too time consuming. (parallel clauses)

3c Word Choice

Word choice makes meaning clear to readers. Specific word choices affect the tone of writing—implying your perception of yourself, your readers, your subject, and your purpose in writing. Consequently, choose words carefully to communicate ideas effectively.

NOUN CLUSTERS

Noun clusters are created when nouns, often in multiples, are used to modify yet another noun. Although the modification patterns may be grammatically correct (nouns *can* function as modifiers), they often create dense clusters of meaning that have to be sorted through carefully.

For example, the phrase *freshman student success ensurance initiative* is overly long, does not read smoothly, and has to be deconstructed. To improve readability, untangle the nouns and place them in easily readable phrases: *an initiative to ensure the success of freshman students.* The reconstructed phrase is easier to interpret than the original and, therefore, communicates the idea more efficiently than does the original.

JARGON

Jargon is the specialized language of a professional group. In some instances, a specific technical term communicates an idea more efficiently than an explanation in everyday language. For instance, the phrase *correlational analyses* explains in two generally understood words a process by which data are both systematically linked and logically compared. However, in many instances, common language that is well selected communicates ideas in a more straightforward and less pretentious way. For example, in many instances the phrase *classroom teacher* communicates an idea with greater clarity and less distraction than the more affected phrase *teacher/practitioner,* which is a stilted way of expressing an idea that is implicit in the word *teacher.*

In your writing, choose words with care. Use technical jargon only when it communicates ideas clearly and efficiently—that is, when it is precise and helpful. Never use jargon to impress because an overreliance on technical terms (especially those that do not communicate ideas precisely and quickly) frustrates readers and clutters prose.

COLLOQUIALISMS

In academic writing, avoid colloquialisms, expressions that are better suited for conversation and other forms of informal communication. Words and phrases such as *write-up* (instead of *report*), *only a few* (rather than *7%*), or *get-together* (in place of *meeting* or *colloquium*) not only lack the specificity of more technical, formal language but also suggest a lack of precision that may make readers question the care with which you have completed your research. For these reasons, use precise, professional language in your writing.

SPECIFICITY

Choose specific words to create clear meaning; do not assume that readers will infer meaning from vague language. For example, rather than writing that a survey contained *numerous questions,* be specific and indicate that it contained *75 questions.* Instead of noting that a study was based on the responses of *many Midwestern students,* describe the research group more precisely: *4,000 freshman students in Indiana, Illinois, Missouri, and Iowa.* Even this description could be made more specific by noting the percentage of male/female respondents, the kinds of schools (liberal arts colleges, small state universities, large state universities, and so on), and the locations of the schools (urban, rural, and so on).

The credibility of research depends on using language that communicates clearly. Consequently, choose words that are as specific as possible.

BIASED LANGUAGE

Whether employed consciously or unconsciously, the use of biased language conveys a writer's insensitivity, ignorance, or, in some instances, prejudice—any of which disrupts communication because readers expect to find balance and fairness in what they read. Writing that incorporates biased language reflects badly on the writer, alienates thoughtful readers, and consequently interferes with effective communication.

As a writer, you should make a concerted effort to use accurate, equitable language. Recognizing that your potential readers represent a broad spectrum of society, choose words with care and avoid stereotypes.

Racial and Ethnic Bias

Language that is racially and ethnically biased often relies on dated words related to racial or ethnic groups. In other instances, racially and ethnically biased word choices ignore the distinct groups that exist within larger classifications, thereby perpetuating broad stereotypes. Consequently, it is preferable to refer to racial or ethnic groups as specifically as possible. (See box, page 57.)

Gender Bias

Language based on stereotypical gender roles—also called *sexist language*—implies through choices of nouns, pronouns, and adjectives that people fall into preassigned roles. Because gender-biased language fails to reflect the diversity of contemporary society, it is inaccurate. Replace nouns that imply gender exclusivity—for example, *chairman* or *spokesman*—with words whose gender-meanings are neutral *(chairperson* or *spokesperson).*

Avoid using gender-specific pronouns when their antecedents are not gender specific. The most common concern is the generic use of a masculine pronoun *(he, him, his, himself)* as in this sentence: "A psychiatrist is bound by professional oath to keep his patients' records confidential." Although this usage was once acceptable, today's writers and readers expect pronoun use to be

Preferred Racial or Ethnic Terms

Questionable	Preferred terms for American citizens	Preferred terms for non-American citizens
Arab	Arab American; *or* Saudi American, Iraqi American, Afghan American, etc.	Saudi, Iraqi, Afghan, etc.
Hispanic	Latino/Latina, Chicano/Chicana; *or* Mexican American, Cuban American, etc.	Mexican, Cuban, Puerto Rican, etc.
Indian	Native American; *or* Cherokee, Ogallala Sioux, Seminole, etc.	Mesoamerican, Inuit, etc.
Black	African American; *or* Kenyan American, Ugandan American, etc.	African; *or* Ugandan, Kenyan, etc.
White	European American; *or* Italian American, French American, Irish American, etc.	Caucasian, European; *or* German, French, Hungarian, Russian, etc.
Oriental	Asian American; *or* Japanese American, Korean American, Chinese American, etc.	Asian; *or* Korean, Japanese, Vietnamese, etc.

inclusive, not exclusionary. Solutions include using alternate pronouns ("A psychiatrist is bound by professional oath to keep his or her patients' records confidential."), plural forms ("Psychiatrists are bound by professional oath to keep their patients' records confidential."), and omission of the pronoun when no confusion is likely ("A psychiatrist is bound by professional oath to keep patients' records confidential.").

Avoid using gender-related adjectives when other modifiers create similar meaning without bias or when gender is not an issue: "The male nurse was both competent and friendly, reassuring the patient and family members" is better presented this way: "The nurse was both competent and friendly, reassuring the patient and family members."

Other Forms of Bias

Be sensitive to the ways in which your language characterizes people by age, class, religion, region, physical and mental ability, or sexual orientation. Do your word choices create stereotypical impressions that disrupt your discussions? Do they convey unintended but negative feelings? Will they offend potential readers and therefore distract them from your ideas? Examine your writing carefully for instances of these kinds of bias and explore alternative ways to convey your meaning.

4 Preparing the Reference List and In-Text Citations

The reference list provides comprehensive information on each of the sources used in a paper. By listing the author or authors, publication dates, full titles, and information about publishers (producers or distributors or Web sites), writers ensure that readers can locate sources for further study.

Sources that appear on the reference list must be cited in the paper using parallel information. For example, if a reference-list entry includes two authors, then the in-text citation must also include both authors' names (see "In-Text Citations" later in this chapter). For this reason, writers should prepare reference-list entries for sources before writing the paper.

This chapter includes detailed discussions of the information required for and the formatting requirements of the reference list; chapters 5–8 provide explanations and examples of the most commonly used sources for APA papers. In addition, this book includes some sources that are not traditionally used in APA journal articles (the writing done by professionals) but that are potentially useful for students' writing; the principles of APA documentation style have been applied in preparing these sample entries.

4a The Reference List — An Overview

A reference list is an alphabetically arranged list of sources used in a paper. It starts on a new page immediately after the last text page of the paper, continues the page numbering, and is also double-spaced. It is introduced by the word *References* (centered but not italicized); if the reference list continues on a second page, no additional heading is required. Entries in the reference list follow the formats described in this chapter. (See pages 117 and 125 for the reference lists of the sample papers.)

4b   Information for APA Entries

Entries for the reference list vary because of the different information they include. All, however, must follow an established order for presenting information:

1. *Authors (and editors).* Take the name or names from the first page of an article or from the title page of a book. Authors' or editors' names are listed in the order in which they appear (not alphabetical order), and initials are used instead of first or middle names. The names of group, institutional, or organizational authors are spelled out completely.

2. *Publication dates.* For professional journals and books, include the publication year in parentheses. For sources that use more specific dates—such as popular magazines, newspapers, television broadcasts, Web sites—include the year and the month or the year, month, and day in parentheses. If a source has no author, the entry begins with the title, followed by the date.

3. *Titles.* List titles completely, taking information from the first page of an article or from the title page of a book. Include both titles and subtitles, no matter how long they are.

4. *Additional information.* Include any of the following information in the order presented here if it is listed on the first page of the article, essay, chapter, or other subsection or the title page of the book: translator, edition number, volume number, issue number (if the journal is paginated separately by issue), and inclusive pages.

5. *Facts of publication.* For periodicals, take the volume number, issue number (if needed), and date from the first few pages in journals and magazines, often in combination with the table of contents, or from the masthead (a listing of information at the top of the first page of newspapers). For books, take the publisher's name from the title page and the date from the copyright page (which immediately follows the title page). Use the publisher's name in abbreviated form (see chapters 5–8 for samples within entries and Appendix C for a list of shortened names for familiar publishers). Include the first city listed with the publisher if more than one is given, an abbreviation for the state or the full

name of the country (see the box below for cities that may be listed without clarification, and see Appendix B for state abbreviations), and the most recent date.

6. *Retrieval information.* For electronic sources, record the date on which you accessed the information, the full name of the source, and the electronic address (URL).

Cities That Are Listed Without Clarification

U.S. cities *(no state required)*	*Other cities* *(no country required)*	
Baltimore	Amsterdam	Stockholm
Boston	Jerusalem	Tokyo
Chicago	London	Vienna
Los Angeles	Milan	
New York	Moscow	
Philadelphia	Paris	
San Francisco	Rome	

4c Format for APA Entries

To ensure easy reading, entries for the reference list must follow this format:

- *Indention patterns.* Begin the first line of each entry at the left margin; indent subsequent lines five spaces (one "Tab" or "Indent").

- *Authors' names.* Because entries must be arranged in alphabetical order, invert all authors' names *(Perrin, R.)* and use an ampersand *(&)*, not the word *and*, to join the names of multiple authors *(Perrin, R., & Taylor, J.)*.

- *Authorless sources.* When no author is identified, list the source by title. Alphabetize a reference-list entry that begins with a title by using the primary words of the title (excluding *a*, *an*, or *the*).

- *Article titles.* Include full titles but capitalize only the first words of titles and subtitles and any proper nouns and proper adjectives; all other words are lowercase.

Article titles use no special punctuation in a reference-list entry (although they are placed in quotation marks in in-text citations and in the paper).

- *Periodical titles.* Capitalize all major words in the titles of periodicals. Follow the title with a comma and then the volume number. Italicize the title *and* volume number, including the separating comma and the comma that follows the volume number.

- *Titles of books.* Capitalize only the first words of titles and subtitles and any proper nouns and proper adjectives; all other words are lowercase. The title is italicized.

- *Publishers' names.* Shorten the names of commercial publishers by using only the main elements of their names (*Houghton,* not *Houghton Mifflin*) and by dropping descriptive titles *(Publishers, Company, Incorporated).* (For samples of shortened forms of publishers' names, see Appendix C.) However, list university presses and organizations and corporations that serve as publishers completely, using the words *Books* and *Press* whenever they are part of an academic publisher's name *(Oxford University Press, American Psychological Association, Northwestern Mutual).*

- *Punctuation within entries.* Separate major sections of entries (author, date, title, and publication information) with periods, including elements enclosed in parentheses or brackets; the period used with the abbreviation of authors' first or middle names substitutes for this period. However, separate the place of publication from the publisher's name with a colon. When an entry ends with a URL, no period is required to close the entry.

- *Spacing within entries.* One space separates elements in APA entries. However, when a journal pages issues separately, the issue number (in parentheses) follows the volume number without a space.

- *Abbreviations.* Use abbreviations for standard parts of periodicals, books, and other print materials. (See the box below for a list of acceptable abbreviations.)

- *Page numbers.* When citing articles in periodicals or chapters or other portions of complete works, list numbers completely (*176–179,* not *176–9* or *176–79*). Journals and magazines list only page numbers; however, page references for newspapers, books, and other print materials use the abbreviations *p.* (for *page*) and *pp.* (for *pages*). No commas are used to separate digits of numbers one thousand or larger when citing pages *(pp. 1295–1298)*. When articles appear on nonconsecutive pages, list them all, separated by commas *(34–35, 38, 54–55, 57, 59)*.

• *Line spacing.* The reference list is double-spaced.

Acceptable Abbreviations

chapter	chap.
edition	ed.
Editor (Editors)	Ed. (Eds.)
no date	n.d.
Number	No.
page (pages)	p. (pp.)
Part	Pt.
Revised edition	Rev. ed.
second edition	2nd ed.
Supplement	Suppl.
Technical Report	Tech. Rep.
Translator	Trans.
Volume	Vol.
volumes	vols.

4d Alphabetizing the Reference List

The reference list must be in alphabetical order, which seems simple enough. Reality often proves more complicated, however, so follow the guidelines in the box on page 64.

4e In-Text Citations

APA documentation has two areas of emphasis: (1) the authors of source materials and (2) the year in which sources were published or presented. This pattern is commonly described as the author-date style.

Circumstances	Rule and sample
Letter-by-letter style	Alphabetize one letter at a time: *Baker, R. L.* precedes *Baker, W. S.; Our American Heritage* comes before *Our American Legacy*
"Nothing precedes something"	The space that follows a name supersedes the letters that follow: *Wood, T. S.* precedes *Woodman, K. F.*
Prefixes	Prefixes are alphabetized as they appear, not as if they appeared in full form: *MacDonald, J. B.* precedes *McDonald, B. V.*
Names with prepositions	Names that incorporate prepositions are alphabetized as if they were spelled closed: *Dean, L. G.* precedes *De Forest, A. M.* (Consult a dictionary regarding patterns for names in different languages.)
Multiple works by the same author	Arrange selections in chronological order: *Sparks, C. G. (1999)* precedes *Sparks, C. G. (2000)*
Single-author and multiple-author works	Single-author works precede multiple-author works: *Kelly, M. J.* precedes *Kelly, M. J., & Dorfman, P. G.*
Groups, institutions, or organizations as authors	Alphabetize group, institutional, or organizational authors by major words in their completely spelled-out names (omitting *a, an,* or *the*): *American Psychological Association* precedes *Anderson, V. W.*
Authorless works	Authorless works are alphabetized by the first significant words in their titles (omitting *a, an,* or *the*): *The price of poverty* precedes *Stewart, R. P.*

When incorporating information from a source, provide an in-text citation that includes, at minimum, the author's last name and the year of publication or presentation. The complexity of some sources requires the inclusion of additional information.

PATTERNS FOR IN-TEXT CITATIONS

An in-text citation (also called a parenthetical note) corresponds to an entry in the reference list at the end of the paper. The information in an entry for the reference list determines what information appears in a citation in the text. For example, if a reference-list entry for a book begins with the author's name, then the author's name appears in the in-text citation. If a reference-list citation for a book begins with the title, however, then the title (or a shortened version of it) appears in the in-text citation. If these correlations are clear and consistent, readers can turn from the paper's in-text citation to the reference list and readily locate the full entry for the source.

BASIC FORMS OF IN-TEXT CITATIONS

To avoid disrupting the text, in-text citations briefly identify only the name of the author or the title under which the source appears in the reference list and give only the year of publication (even when reference-list entries require month or month and day). For the sake of clarity and smoothness, you may incorporate some of the necessary information in your sentences. For example:

> Survivors also have a higher than normal chance of dying. For example, widows and widowers have a forty percent higher chance of death during the first six months after losing a spouse than other people their age (Backer, Hannon, & Gregg, 1994).

OR

> Survivors also have a higher than normal chance of dying. Backer, Hannon, and Gregg (1994) explain that widows and widowers have a forty percent higher chance of death during the first six months after losing a spouse than other people their age.

Reference-list entry

Backer, B., Hannon, N., & Gregg, J. Y. (1994). *To listen, to comfort, to care: Reflections on death and dying.* Albany: NY: Delmar.

In special cases, the rule of using only the author's name and the date is superseded:

Special circumstance	*Rule and sample*
Two authors with the same last name	Include initials and last name: (Barratt, J., 1999), distinct from (Barratt, L., 1998).
Multiple works by the same author (same year)	Use letters to distinguish the sources: (Morrison, 2000a), distinct from (Morrison, 2000b). The letters indicate the alphabetical order of the titles.
Two authors	Use both last names, joined by an ampersand: (Scott & Fuller, 1997).
Three, four, or five authors	The *first* notation includes all names (Jarnow, Judelle, & Guerriro, 2001). *Subsequent* citations, except as noted, use the first author's name and *et al.,* not italicized: (Jarnow et al., 2001). Further references within a single paragraph omit the date: (Jarnow et al.).
Six or more authors	Use the first author's name and *et al.,* not italicized: (Gershey et al., 1995).
Organization as author	In the first note, present the organization's name in full, with an abbreviation in brackets: (National Council of Teachers of English [NCTE], 1999). Use the shortened form in subsequent notations: (NCTE, 1999).

No author	Include a shortened version of the title, appropriately capitalized and punctuated, and the year: ("Optimum Performance from Test Subjects," 1999); (*Common Ground*, 1986).
Multiple publication dates	Include both dates, separated by a slash: (Jagger & Richards, 1994/2001).
Reference works	List by author if applicable (Angermüller, 1998) or by a shortened form of the title ("Manhattan Project," 1998).
Two or more works by the same author (same note)	To cite several works by the same author (all included in the reference list), include the author's name and all dates in chronological order, separated by commas: (Vidich, 1997, 1998, 2001).
Two or more works by different authors (same note)	To cite several works by different authors in the same note, list each author (in alphabetical order) and date, separated by semicolons: (Bennet, 1996; Greene, 2000; Swift, 1999).
Parts of sources	To cite only a portion of a source, include the author or title as appropriate, the date, and clarifying information: (Thomas, 2001, p. 451); (Spindrell, 2000, chaps. 2–3).
Personal communication Note: Although cited in the text, personal communications do not have entries in the reference list.	Cite e-mail and other correspondence, memos, interviews, and so on by listing the person's name, the clarifying phrase *personal communication* (not italicized), and the specific date (Bates, L., personal communication, June 7, 2002).

4f Quotations

When an author's manner of expression is unique or when his or her ideas or language are difficult to paraphrase or summarize, quote the passage in your text. To avoid plagiarism, quoted material must be reproduced word for word—including exact spelling and punctuation—and must be properly separated from your text and accurately cited.

The pattern for incorporating a quotation varies depending on the length of the quotation. In-text citations for quotations also include a specific page reference.

BRIEF QUOTATIONS (FEWER THAN FORTY WORDS)

A quotation of fewer than forty words appears within a normal paragraph, with the author's words enclosed in quotation marks. The in-text citation, placed in parentheses, follows the closing quotation mark. It includes the author's name and the publication date (unless they have been previously mentioned in the text), as well as a specific page reference, introduced with the abbreviation *p.* or *pp.* (not italicized). For example:

> Awards shows are now being subsumed by the unsavory business of movie finance: "Movie studios love a good fight, and a bad one too. But the Oscar battles have become trench warfare and dirty tricks" (Corliss, 2002, p. 60).

OR

> Awards shows are now being subsumed by the unsavory business of movie finance. Richard Corliss (2002) observed that "movie studios love a good fight, and a bad one too. But the Oscar battles have become trench warfare and dirty tricks" (p. 60).

Reference-list entry

Corliss, R. (2002, March 25). Inside the Oscar wars. *Time, 159,* 60–62.

LONG QUOTATIONS (FORTY OR MORE WORDS)

A quotation of forty or more words is set off from a normal paragraph in an indented block paragraph. After introducing the quotation, start the quotation on a new line, indented five spaces (use the "Indent" feature to maintain the five-space indention throughout the quotation). Quotation marks do not appear at the opening and closing of a block quotation. Like the surrounding text, the quotation is also double-spaced. Note that the period precedes the in-text citation with a block quotation. For example:

> Anthropologists and social scientists now realize that a broader range of information must be collected for us to understand the diversity of ethnic and social groups:
>
>> Family histories that reveal the dynamics of intergenerational relationships in all of their dimensions (education, economic, psychological)—the constant mentoring and tutoring, the patience of grandmothers with grandbabies—must be collected. We need as researchers to collect data that avoid the patronizing "we" (urban professionals) who know what is best for "you" or "them" (the poor people). (Halperin, 1994, p. 196)
>
> Current studies, as a result, are developed in a multidimensional way.

OR

> Anthropologists and social scientists now realize that a broader range of information must be collected for us to understand the diversity of ethnic and social groups. Rhoda H. Halperin (1994) offered this rationale:
>
>> Family histories that reveal the dynamics of intergenerational relationships in all of their dimensions (education, economic, psychological)—the constant mentoring and tutoring, the patience of grandmothers with grandbabies—must be collected. We need as researchers to collect data that avoid the patronizing "we" (urban professionals) who know what is best for "you" or "them" (the poor people). (p. 196)
>
> Current studies, as a result, are developed in a multidimensional way.

Reference-list entry

Halperin, R. H. (1994). Appalachians in cities: Issues and challenges in research. In K. M. Borman & P. J. Obermiller
(Eds.), *Mountains to metropolis: Appalachian migrants
in American cities* (pp. 181–197). Westport, CT: Bergin.

PUNCTUATION WITH QUOTATIONS

Single quotation marks. To indicate an author's use of
quotation marks within a brief quotation (which is set off
by double quotation marks), change the source's punctuation to single quotation marks, as in this example:

> Joel Kotkin (1993) emphasized the influence of immi-
> grants in American culture and business: "Even blue
> denim jeans, the 'uniform' of the gold rush—and
> indeed, the American West—owe their origination
> and name to Levi Strauss, a gold rush-era immigrant
> to San Francisco" (p. 57).

Reference-list entry

Kotkin, J. (1994). *How race, religion, and identity determine
success in the new global economy.* New York: Random.

Because long block quotations do not begin and end with
quotation marks, the source's quotation marks remain
double, as in this example:

> James Sellers (1991) suggested that self-identity is
> often inextricably linked to an individual's nationality:
>> The United States is the "oldest new nation," we
>> are often told by political scientists; and the
>> national heritage, while it has certainly not turned
>> out to be a "melting pot," has become a power-
>> ful background influence upon the identity of
>> Americans, reshaping even the ways in which they
>> express their ethnicity or religion. (p. 97)
> Whatever our race, religion, or ethnicity are, we are,
> perhaps, most obviously, Americans.

Reference-list entry

Sellers, J. (1994). *Essays in American ethics.* New York: Lang.

Brackets. Use brackets to indicate that you have added
words for clarity within a quotation. Most often, the

words you add are specific nouns to substitute for pronouns that are vague outside the context of the original
work. However, you may substitute a different tense of
the same verb (for example, *used* for *use*).

> Michael Spagat (1994) explained that in some indus-
> tries workers receive more wages than the wealth they
> create; consequently, "if [value-destroying industries]
> were closed down, money would be saved but the sav-
> ings would not be enough to pay full unemployment
> compensation" (p. 52).

Reference-list entry

Spagat, M. (1994). The disintegration of the Russian
economy. In D. W. Blum (Ed.), *Russia's future:
Consolidation or disintegration?* (pp. 47–67). Boulder,
CO: Westview.

Ellipsis points. Use ellipsis points—three spaced periods—to indicate where words have been omitted within
a quotation. To indicate an omission at the beginning or
end of a sentence, retain the sentence's punctuation
(producing four spaced periods).

> Robert I. Williams (1993) stressed the social dimensions
> of comedy in this way: "Humor is a guide. It is largely
> culture bound. Chinese Communist jokes do not do
> well here, just as ours tend to be duds in Beijing. . . . Yet
> there is a range of humor that works for a broad, varie-
> gated audience. The very existence of comic films is
> testimony" (pp. 56–57).

[Omitted: "The humor of a Chicago street gang will not
work in a retirement home, even one in Chicago.
Regional, age, gender, and social differences all enter in."]

Reference-list entry

Williams, R. I. (1994). *Comic practice: Comic response.*
Newark, DE: University of Delaware Press.

5 Citing Periodicals

Journals, most often affiliated with professional organizations, are scholarly publications whose articles are subjected to careful review. Often called refereed journals, they are the mainstay of much research because they present ideas and information developed by scholars and specialists—and reviewed by scholars—for an audience of scholars. Magazines, by contrast, are commercial publications that present ideas and information for general readers who are nonspecialists; they provide nontechnical discussions and general reactions to issues. Newspapers—published daily or weekly—provide nearly instantaneous reactions to issues in primary stories and more reflective discussions in editorials and featured articles. These periodicals provide recent discussions of ideas and issues, as well as reports of research of importance to writers of researched papers.

To cite periodicals in a reference list, follow the guidelines given in this chapter.

5a An Article in a Journal with Continuous Paging

A journal with continuous paging numbers an entire year's worth of journals consecutively, even though there are separately numbered issues. For example, *Educational Psychologist*'s volume 37 (representing 2002) has numbered issues that are continuously paged: issue number 1 (winter 2002) includes pages 1–66, number 2 (spring 2002) spans pages 67–136, number 3 (summer 2002) continues with pages 137–196, and so on.

When an article comes from a journal with continuous paging, list its authors first, followed by the year of publication and the title of the article. Next, include the title of the journal (with all major words capitalized), a comma, the volume number, and another comma (all italicized). Finish the entry by including the inclusive page numbers, without a page abbreviation.

Nussbaum, J. F., & Bettini, L. M. (1994). Shared stories of the grandparent–grandchild relationship. *The International Journal of Aging and Human Development, 39,* 67–80.

> ***In-text citation***   (Nussbaum & Bettini, 1994)

Trigo, B. (2000). Thinking subjectivity in Latin American criticism. *Revista de Estudious Hispánicos, 34,* 309–329.

> ***In-text citation***   (Trigo, 2000)

5b An Article in a Journal with Separate Paging

A journal with separate paging begins each numbered issue with page 1, even though a year's worth of journals is assigned a single volume number. For example, *English Journal*'s volume 91 (representing 2001/2002) has numbered issues, each of which has separate paging: issue number 1 (September 2001) includes pages 1–136, issue number 2 (November 2001) spans pages 1–132, issue number 3 (January 2002) covers pages 1–144, and so on.

When a journal has separate paging for each issue, follow the volume number with the issue number, in parentheses; no space separates the volume from the issue, and the issue number is not italicized. All other information in the entry is the same as in a entry for a journal with continuous paging.

Graves, D. (2000). Multiculturalism and the choral canon: 1975–2000. *Choral Journal, 41*(2), 37–44.

> ***In-text citation***　(Graves, 2000)

Lewis, J. (2000). "We do not ask you to condone this": How the blacklist saved Hollywood. *Cinema Journal, 39*(2), 3–30.

> ***In-text citation***　(Lewis, 2000)

5c　An Abstract

Although writers most often refer to entire articles, in very special circumstances (for example, when an abstract's summary of key principles is succinct or quotable), you may want to cite only the abstract. In those rare instances, first prepare a full citation of the article; however, insert the word *Abstract*, not italicized, within brackets after the article's title. The period that normally follows the title follows the closing bracket. The page reference is to the abstract only, not the entire article.

Winkler, I., Korzyukov, O., Gumenyuk, V., Cowan, N., Linkenkaer-Hansen, K., Ilmonieni, R. J., et al. (2002). Temporary and longer term retention of acoustic information [Abstract]. *Psychophysiology, 39*, 530.

> ***In-text citation***　(Winkler et al., 2002)

For a work with multiple authors, cite only the first six; then use the abbreviate *et al.*, not italicized, to refer to the other authors. In the preceding example, two additional authors' names are not used. Notice that in the in-text citation, only the first author's name is used.

Hedden, T., & Zhang, J. (2002). What do you think I think you think? Strategic reasoning in matrix games [Abstract]. *Cognition, 85*, 1.

> ***In-text citation***　(Hedden & Zhang, 2000)

5d An Article in a Monthly Magazine

An article from a monthly magazine is listed by author. The date is given by year and month, separated by a comma, in parentheses. The article title appears without special punctuation. The title of the magazine, however, is presented with all major words capitalized, followed by a comma, the volume number, and another comma (all italicized). The entry ends with inclusive page numbers listed without page abbreviations.

If no author is listed with the article, begin with the article's title, followed by the date and magazine title.

Furlow, B. (2000, October). The uses of crying and begging. *Natural History, 109,* 62–67.

In-text citation   (Furlow, 2000)

Apocalypse later. (1995, May). *Discover, 16,* 20.

In-text citation   ("Apocalypse Later," 1995)

Note that the title in the in-text citation uses full capitalization and quotation marks.

5e An Article in a Weekly Magazine

The entry for a weekly magazine is presented just as that for a monthly magazine is, with one important difference: The day (along with the year and month) is included in parentheses. In the corresponding in-text citation, however, only the year is required.

Gest, T. (2000, October 9). Fixing your school. *U.S. News and World Report, 129,* 65–67.

In-text citation   (Gest, 2000)

Hentoff, N. (1990, March 12). The constitutionalist [profile of Justice William Brennan]. *The New Yorker, 66,* 45–46, 48, 52, 54, 56–70.

In-text citation   (Hentoff, 1990)

When pages are not sequential, list them all, according to the pattern presented in the preceding sample. Notice that clarifying information has been added in brackets and that the article *The* is included in the magazine's title.

5f An Article in a Newspaper

An entry for a newspaper article resembles that for a magazine, except that paging is indicated with a page abbreviation (*p.* or *pp.,* not italicized), and section numbers or letters are included. The page abbreviation precedes the page and section numbers.

Zeleny, J. (2000, January 17). Election reform is popular, political—and pricey. *The Chicago Tribune,* p. 2:1.

> ***In-text citation*** (Zeleny, 2000)

When newspaper sections are numbered, a colon is used to separate the section (section 2, in the sample above) from the page number (page 1 of section 2, in the sample above).

Eckstrom, K. (2000, December 30). A year of front-page faith. *The Washington Post,* p. B9.

> ***In-text citation*** (Eckstrom, 2000)

When sections are indicated by letters, they are presented along with the page numbers, with no intervening punctuation or space.

5g An Article in a Newsletter

The entry for an article in a newsletter follows the pattern for a magazine: the author, date, title of selection, title of newsletter, volume number, and inclusive pages (without page abbreviations). Because newsletters often appear seasonally, include such identifying information along with the year.

Neuenschwander, J. A. (2001, Winter). *Oral history as evidence. OHA [Oral History Association] Newsletter, 35,* 1, 4–5.

> ***In-text citation*** (Neuenschwander, 2001)

To provide additional clarity, the full version of an acronym (*OHA* in the sample) may be enclosed in brackets.

Davis, A. (2001, September). Promoting equality in our schools: Teaching beyond tolerating, and toward respecting differences. *The Social Studies Professional, 164,* 1, 7.

> ***In-text citation*** (Davis, 2001)

5h   An Editorial

The entry for an editorial—an opinion-based essay—resembles that for a magazine or newspaper article, with one exception: The word *Editorial* (not italicized) is placed within brackets immediately after the title of the essay, if there is one. The period that normally follows the title follows the closing bracket.

Donlan, T. G. (1995, January 2). Of babies and bathwater: Tax cuts are nice, but America really needs tax reform [Editorial]. *Barron's, 75,* 43.

> **In-text citation**   (Donlan, 1995)

Herbert B. (2001, January 1). Addicted to guns [Editorial]. *The New York Times,* p. A17.

> **In-text citation**   (Herbert, 2001)

5i   A Letter to the Editor

Following the author's name and the publication date, include the phrase *Letter to the editor* (not italicized) in brackets, followed by a period. The rest of the entry follows the pattern appropriate for the periodical.

Hancock, T. (2000, January). [Letter to the editor]. *Harper's, 300,* 6.

> **In-text citation**   (Hancock, 2000)

Mogavero, M. A. (1995, January 16). [Letter to the editor]. *Business Week,* 11.

> **In-text citation**   (Mogavero, 1995)

Business Week does not use volume numbers, so none can be listed.

5j   A Review

After the author, date, and review title (if there is one), include a descriptive phrase that begins "Review of the book (film, record, car, computer game)" and ends with the specific product name; enclose this information in brackets, followed by a period. Then continue the entry as is appropriate for the source.

Cocks, J. (2001, January 8). Fascinating rhythm [Review of the television series *Jazz*]. *Time, 157,* 69, 72.

> ***In-text citation***   (Cocks, 2001)

Travers, P. (1995, January 26). Legends for the mall [Review of the film *Legends of the fall*]. *Rolling Stone,* 65–66.

> ***In-text citation***   (Travers, 1995)

Rolling Stone does not use volume numbers, so none can be listed.

5k   An Abstract from *Dissertation Abstracts International*

This specialized entry requires the author's name, the year in parentheses, and the title of the dissertation (without special punctuation). In parentheses, include the phrase *Doctoral dissertation* (not italicized), the degree-granting university, and the year of completion—all separated with commas. Follow the ending parenthesis with a period. Close the entry by identifying *Dissertation Abstracts International* (italicized), followed by the volume number and a comma (also italicized), and the dissertation's identification number.

Andrews, K. T. (1998). "Freedom is a constant struggle": The dynamics and consequences of the Mississippi civil rights movement: 1960–1984. (Doctoral dissertation, State University of New York at Stony Brook, 1998). *Dissertation Abstracts International, 59,* AAT9824679.

> ***In-text citation***   (Andrews, 1998)

Mellencamp, A. V. (1992). Teacher receptivity to change: The importance of voice. (Doctoral dissertation, University of Vermont, 1992). *Dissertation Abstracts International, 53,* 1752A.

> ***In-text citation***   (Mellencamp, 1992)

5l   A Secondary Source

The authors of primary sources report their own research and ideas; the authors of secondary sources report the research and ideas of others. For example, Wise, Smead, and Hueber (1987) conducted and reported a study on crisis intervention; it is a primary source. In 2002, Allen, Jerome, White, Marston, Lamb, Pope, and Rawlins incorporated material from the original article in an article for *Psychology in the Schools;* it is a secondary source. Although it is best to use the original or primary source (Wise, Smead, and Hueber), at times you must use the secondary source (Allen et al.).

If you cite material that appears in a secondary source, the reference-list entry must be for *the source you used,* not the original (even though you might be able to secure full documentation from the secondary source's reference list); for ethical reasons, you must cite the source that was part of your research. Therefore, refer to the original source in the text of the paper. In the in-text citation, however, clarify the use of the original material with the phrase *as cited in* (not italicized). Provide an entry for the secondary source you used in the reference list.

Allen, M., Jerome, A., White, A., Marston, S., Lamb, S., Pope, D., et al. (2002). The preparation of school psychologists for crisis intervention. *Psychology in the Schools, 39,* 427–439.

Wise, Smead, and Hueber's 1987 study on crisis intervention and personnel training (as cited in Allen et al., 2002) adds further dimension to the discussion.

Books provide comprehensive, extended discussions of topics. Those published by scholarly or university presses are often targeted to specialists in particular fields and provide a broad range of technical information and complex analyses. Those published by trade (commercial) publishers often are directed to nonspecialists.

Because books take several years to produce, they often provide reflective interpretations that have the benefit of critical distance. Consequently, they provide balance in research. To cite books in a reference list, follow the guidelines in this chapter.

6a   A Book by One Author

The entry for a book by a single author begins with his or her name, followed by the year in parentheses, the title, the city and state, and the publisher. Only the first word and proper nouns and proper adjectives of a book title are capitalized; the title is italicized.

Monmonier, M. (1999). *Air apparent: How meteorologists learned to map, predict, and dramatize weather.* Chicago: University of Chicago Press.

> **In-text citation**   (Monmonier, 1999)

University and *Press* are spelled out in the preceding sample because the publisher has a university affiliation.

Nader, R. (1965). *Unsafe at any speed: The designed-in danger of the American automobile.* New York: Grossman.

> **In-text citation**   (Nader, 1965)

Notice that *American,* a proper adjective, is capitalized in the title, although other words are not. *Grossman,* a commercial publisher, is listed in its briefest recognizable form.

6b   A Book by Two or More Authors

When a book has multiple authors, their names appear in the order presented on the title page, not alphabetical order. The names of two to six authors are listed, with all of their names inverted. An ampersand (&) joins the last two names in the series. If a book has more than six authors, the first six are listed completely, followed by the abbreviation *et al.* (Latin for *and others*), not italicized.

Freedman, D., Pisani, R., Purves, R., & Adhikari, A. (1991).
Statistics (2nd ed.). New York: Norton.

> **First in-text citation** (Freedman, Pisani, Purves, &
> Adhikari, 1991)

> **Second and subsequent citations** (Freedman et al., 1991)

Kegley, C. W., & Raymond, G. A. (1999). *How nations make
peace*. New York: St. Martin's.

> **In-text citation** (Kegley & Raymond, 1999)

6c A Book with No Author Named

When no author or editor is named, list the book by title.
When an editor is listed, begin the entry with the editor's
name.

*United Press International stylebook: The authoritative
handbook for writers, editors, and news directors*
(3rd ed.). (1992). Lincolnwood, IL: National.

> **In-text citation** (*United Press International*, 1992)

The preceding source is listed by title. *United Press
International* has each word capitalized because it is an
organization. With an authorless book, the edition number
follows the title, in parentheses; notice that the edition
number above is not italicized and that the period that
normally follows the title follows the closing parenthesis
instead. The year follows the edition number. See the
section "An Edition Other Than the First" for the common
pattern of presenting editions.

Swanton, M. J. (Ed.). (1990). *An Anglo-Saxon chronicle*.
Exeter, England: University of Exeter Press.

> **In-text citation** (Swanton, 1990)

This source is listed by editor. In this sample, the country
is also listed.

6d A Book with an Organization as Author

When an organization is listed as the author, spell out
the name completely in the author position. When the

organization is also the publisher, use the word *Author*, not italicized, in the publisher position.

American Medical Association. (1989). *Manual of style* (8th ed.). Baltimore: Williams.

> **First in-text citation**   (American Medical Association [AMA], 1989)
>
> **Second and subsequent citations**   (AMA, 1989)

American Psychological Association. (2001). *Publication manual of the American Psychological Association* (5th ed.). Washington, DC: Author.

> **First in-text citation**   (American Psychological Association [APA], 2001)
>
> **Second and subsequent citations**   (APA, 2001)

6e   An Edition Other Than the First

The edition number, which appears on the title page, follows the title of the book, in parentheses. Note that it is not italicized and that the period that normally follows the title follows the closing parenthesis instead.

Gillespie, J. T., & Naden, C. T. (1994). *Best books for children: Preschool through grade 6* (5th ed.). New York: Bowker.

> **In-text citation**   (Gillespie & Naden, 1994)

Terril, R. J. (1999). *World criminal justice systems: A survey* (4th ed.). Cincinnati, OH: Anderson.

> **In-text citation**   (Terril, 1999)

6f   An Edited Collection

Present an entire edited collection like a traditional book, with the editor's name in the author position.

Hartman, G. H. (Ed.). (1994). *Holocaust remembrance: The shapes of memory*. Cambridge, MA: Blackwell.

> **In-text citation**   (Hartman, 1994)

6g   An Original Selection in an Edited Collection

To cite an original selection in an edited collection, begin with the name of the author of the selection, followed by the date in parentheses. The title of the individual selection follows the publication date; no special punctuation is used. Introduced by the preposition *In* (not italicized), the collection editor is listed next (his or her name is in normal order, followed by the abbreviation *Ed.* in parentheses but not italicized), followed by a comma and the title of the collection, italicized. Inclusive page numbers for the selection, with the abbreviation for pages, are listed completely in parentheses, followed by publishing information.

McKnight, R. (1998). Spirituality in the workplace. In J. D.
    Adams (Ed.), *Transforming work* (pp. 160–178). New
    York: Miles River.

   In-text citation   (McKnight, 1998)

6h   A Previously Published Selection in an Edited Collection

When a selection has been reprinted from a work published earlier, provide identifying information in parentheses at the end of the entry. Include the information required for the original source, but note that page numbers appear with the abbreviation for pages, even when the original source is a journal or magazine, and the year follows the page numbers. Also note that the closing parenthesis is not followed by a period.

Ackerman, S. (1999). *The queen mother and the cult in
    ancient Israel.* In A. Bach (Ed.), *Women in the Hebrew
    bible: A reader* (pp. 179–194). New York: Routledge.
    (Reprinted from *The Journal of Biblical Literature,
    112*(3), pp. 385–401, 1993)

   In-text citation   (Ackerman, 1999)

Wallace, M. (1990). Mickey Mouse history: Portraying the
    past at Disney World. In F. Manning & J. M. Philbert
    (Eds.), *Customs in conflict: The anthology of a
    changing world* (pp. 304–332). Peterborough, Ontario,

Canada: Broadview. (Reprinted from *Radical History Review, 32*, pp. 33–55, 1985)

In-text citation   (Wallace, 1990)

Note that provinces are also listed.

6i   A Revised or Enlarged Edition

Enclose the description of a revised or enlarged edition in parentheses following the title. As with other editions, the parenthetical information precedes the period that follows the title, and this information is not italicized.

Hiltz, S. R., & Turoff, M. (1993). *The network nation: Human communication via computer* (Rev. ed.). Cambridge: Massachusetts Institute of Technology Press.

In-text citation   (Hiltz & Turoff, 1993)

In the preceding example, because the state is included in the name of the university press it is not required after the city.

Lau, L. K. (Ed.). (2000). *Distance learning technologies: Issues, trends, and opportunities* (Rev. ed.). Hershey, PA: Idea Group.

In-text citation   (Lau, 2000)

6j   A Reprinted Book

The entry for a reprinted book begins with the full entry of the version you have used; the entry ends with a parenthetical notation that describes the original publication date.

Lubbock, J. (1998). *The choice of books.* Lake Oswego, OR: Blackwell's. (Original work published 1896)

In-text citation   (Lubbock, 1998)

Johnson, A. (1998). *The hidden writer: Diaries and the creative life.* New York: Doubleday. (Original work published 1997)

In-text citation   (Johnson, 1998)

6k A Multivolume Work

When citing a complete multivolume work, the number of volumes appears in parentheses following the title but before the period; volume information is not italicized. When citing a separately titled volume of a multivolume work, list the single volume title, followed by a colon and the specific volume number, followed by a period; then list the title of the multivolume work. The specific title, volume information, and multivolume title are all italicized.

Packard, F. R. (1973). *History of medicine in the United States* (Vols. 1–2). New York: Hafner.

> ***In-text citation***   (Packard, 1973)

The preceding entry refers to a complete two-volume work.

Roberts, J. M. (1999). *The age of revolution: Vol. 7. The illustrated history of the world.* New York: Oxford University Press.

> ***In-text citation***   (Roberts, 1999)

This entry refers to a single volume of a ten-volume collection.

6l An Article in an Encyclopedia or Other Reference Work

To cite an article in an encyclopedia or other reference work, begin with the author's name, when it is available, followed by the date in parentheses. Next list the subject heading under which the material appears (exactly as it appears in the source), without special punctuation. Follow it with the title of the reference work. In parentheses, but before the period that follows the title, include the volume number, if applicable, and inclusive pages. End the entry with the city and state (if required) and publisher.

Angermüller, R. (1980). Salieri, Antonio. In *The new Grove dictionary of music and musicians* (Vol. 16, pp. 415–421). New York: Grove.

> ***In-text citation***   (Angermüller, 1980)

If an article in a reference source has no author, begin with the subject title, followed by the date in parentheses. The rest of the entry follows the normal pattern.

Fluoxetine Hydrochloride [Prozac]. (1995). In *Nursing 96 drug handbook* (pp. 383–384). Springhouse, PA: Springhouse.

    In-text citation ("Fluoxetine Hydrochloride," 1995)

Note that in the in-text citation the article title is enclosed in quotation marks.

6m A Work in a Series

When a book is part of a series, that fact will be stated on the title page. The entry follows the pattern for a similar book, except that the series title (capitalized and italicized) appears in a phrase that immediately precedes the city and publisher.

Sharpe, T. (2000). *Wallace Stevens: A literary life*. In *Literary Life Series*. New York: St. Martin's.

    In-text citation (Sharpe, 2000)

When volumes in a series are numbered, include that information following the series title.

Cather, W. (1996). *My Ántonia*. In *Everyman's Library: Vol. 228*. New York: Knopf.

    In-text citation (Cather, 1996)

6n A Translation

Under most circumstances, the translator of a text is cited in parentheses immediately after the title of the selection (whether it is an essay, chapter, or complete text) but before the closing period for that element.

Beauvoir, S. de. (1991). *The ethics of ambiguity* (B. Frechtman, Trans.). New York: Citadel.

    In-text citation (Beauvoir, 1991)

The preceding entry indicates that Frechtman translated the entire book.

Kiš, D. (1998). Dogs and books (D. Mikic-Mitchell, Trans.).
    In I. Stavans (Ed.), *The Oxford book of Jewish stories*
    (pp. 325–335). New York: Oxford University Press.

> ***In-text citation***   (Kiš, 1998)

This sample indicates that Mikic-Mitchell translated only
the selection presented in this entry. Had she translated
the entire collection, her name would have appeared
after the anthology title.

6o   A Government Document—Committee, Commission, Department

An entry for a government document follows the pattern
used for another similar source. Because many government documents are book-length, that pattern most
often applies. Note, however, that APA style requires a
publication number for a government document, if available (check on the title page or back cover), presented in
parentheses after the title. Also note that *Government
Printing Office* is spelled out, not abbreviated.

Commission on Migrant Education. (1992). *Invisible
    children: A portrait of migrant education in the
    United States* (92-0607-P). Washington, DC:
    Government Printing Office.

> ***In-text citation***   (Commission on Migrant Education, 1992)

Commission on the Assassination of President Kennedy.
    (1964). *Investigation of the assassination of President
    John F. Kennedy: Hearings before the president's
    Commission on the Assassination of President Kennedy*
    (Vols. 1–16). Washington, DC: Government Printing
    Office.

> ***In-text citation***   (Commission on the Assassination of
> President Kennedy, 1964)

6p   A Preface, Introduction, Foreword, Epilogue, or Afterword

Untitled material that is included before the primary text
begins (such as a preface, introduction, or foreword) or
after it (an epilogue or afterword) is cited separately by

providing a descriptive title (within brackets), followed by complete entry information.

Fuller, R. B. (1971). [Introduction]. In V. Papanek, *Design for the real world* (pp. vii–xix). New York: Pantheon.

> *In-text citation* (Fuller, 1971)

The preceding sample shows an introduction written by someone (Fuller) other than the author of the book (Papanek). Notice that page numbers are indicated in lowercase roman numerals, as is often the case with introductory material.

Walburg, Rivka. (1992). [Epilogue]. *A child like that* (pp. 170–177). New York: Feldheim.

> *In-text citation* (Walburg, 1992)

In this entry, the epilogue was written by the author of the book.

6q   A Monograph

To create an entry for a monograph (a separately published, essay-length selection that is sometimes a reprint of a journal article and sometimes an independently prepared selection that is part of a series), include traditional publishing information. However, after the title and in parentheses, include the monograph series title and monograph number.

Wessler, S., & Moss, M. (2001). *Hate crimes on campus: The problem and efforts to confront it.* (Bureau of Justice Assistance Monograph No. 187249). Washington, DC: Bureau of Justice Assistance, Department of Justice.

> *In-text citation* (Wessler & Moss, 2001)

Note that the monograph number is introduced by *No.,* the abbreviation for *number.*

Klein, S., Medrich, E., & Perez-Ferreiro, V. (1996). *Fitting the pieces: Education reform that works.* (Studies in Educational Reform Monograph No. 1). Washington, DC: U.S. Department of Education.

> *In-text citation* (Klein, Medrich, & Perez-Ferreiro, 1996)

6r A Pamphlet or Brochure

When a pamphlet or brochure contains clearly presented information, it is cited like a book, with a descriptive title enclosed in brackets. When information is missing, use these abbreviations: *N.p.* for "No place of publication," *n.p.* for "no publisher," and *n.d.* for "no date." None of these abbreviations is italicized in an entry.

Adams, A. B. (1984). *Hospice care* [Pamphlet]. New York: American Cancer Society.

> ***In-text citation*** (Adams, 1984)

Lyme disease and related disorders [Brochure]. (2000). Groton, NY: Pfizer Company.

> ***In-text citation*** (*Lyme Disease and Related Disorders,* 2000)

6s A Dissertation

The entry for an unpublished dissertation begins with the author's name, the date, and the title, presented in the pattern used for a book. However, the phrase *Unpublished doctoral dissertation* (not italicized) follows, with the degree-granting university and city (and state, province, or country, if required for clarity) completing the entry. Published dissertations are books and should be cited accordingly.

Lehner, L. (1998). *Gravitational radiation from black hole spacetimes.* Unpublished doctoral dissertation. University of Pittsburgh.

> ***In-text citation*** (Lehner, 1998)

Because the city is included in the university name, none is required in the closing of the entry.

Straw, W. O. (1990). *Popular music as a cultural commodity: The American recorded music industries, 1976–1985.* Unpublished doctoral dissertation. McGill University, Montreal, Quebec, Canada.

> ***In-text citation*** (Straw, 1990)

6t   Published Proceedings from a Conference

The published proceedings from a conference present revised, printed versions of papers that were delivered at the meeting. If the proceedings are published individually, cite them as you would books. If they are published regularly, present them as periodicals.

Capitalize the name of the meeting, conference, or symposia. If the title includes the state, province, or country name, do not repeat it in the publishing information.

Le Prohn, N. S. (Ed.). (2002). *Assessing youth behavior using the child behavior checklist in family and children's services. Proceedings from the Child Behavior Checklist Roundtable.* Washington, DC: CWLA.

    In-text citation   (Le Prohn, 2002)

Horgan, T., Tienson, J., & Potrc, M. (Eds.). (2002). *Origins: The common sources of the analytic and phenomenological traditions. Proceedings of the Spindel Conference, University of Memphis. Southern Journal of Philosophy, 40*(Suppl.), 1–279.

    In-text citation   (Horgan, Tienson, & Potrc, 2002)

Notice that *Suppl.,* the abbreviation for *supplement,* follows the journal's volume number, without italics.

6u   An Annual Report

An annual report is normally presented like a book, with the company name in the author position.

Alcan. (2000). *Paving the way to a bright future: Annual report 1999.* New York: Author.

    In-text citation   (Alcan, 2000)

Xerox. (1994). *The document company: 1993 annual report.* Stamford, CT: Author.

    In-text citation   (Xerox, 1994)

6v Multiple Works by the Same Author

When citing several sources by the same author, repeat the name completely each time. Alphabetical order takes precedence, with single authors listed before multiple authors. List works by single authors or by the same multiple authors chronologically. If several works were published in the same year, arrange them alphabetically by title.

Ehrenreich, B. (1999, June). Who needs men? Addressing the prospect of a matrilinear millennium. [Interview]. *Harper's, 298,* 33–46.

Ehrenreich, B. (1999, June 20). Looking to put fatherhood in its proper place. *The New York Times,* p. L14.

Ehrenreich, B. (2000, May 8). Barefoot, pregnant, and ready to fight. *Time, 156,* 62.

Ehrenreich, B., Hess, E., & Jacobs, G. (1986). *Re-making love: The feminization of sex.* Garden City, NY: Anchor-Doubleday.

Alternative in-text citations

- The *Harper's* article: (Ehrenreich, 1999a)
- The *Times* article: (Ehrenreich, 1999b)
- All three single-author works in the same citation: (Ehrenreich, 1999a, 1999b, 2000)
- The multiple-author book: (Ehrenreich, Hess, & Jacobs, 1986)

Ehrenreich's three separately written works appear first, arranged in chronological order. The Ehrenreich, Hess, and Jacobs book follows.

6w A Secondary Source

The authors of primary sources report their own research and ideas; the authors of secondary sources report the research and ideas of others. For example, Collier conducted studies on the feeding habits of rats, which he reported in an article; it is a primary source. In 2001, Staddon incorporated material from the original article in his book *Adaptive Dynamics: The Theoretical Analysis of Behavior;* it is a secondary source. Although it is best to use the original or primary source (Collier), sometimes you must use the secondary source (Staddon.).

If you cite material that appears in a secondary source, the reference-list entry must be for *the source you used,* not the original (even though you might be able to secure full documentation from the secondary source's reference list); you must ethically cite the source that was part of your research. Therefore, refer to the original source in the text of the paper. In the in-text citation, however, clarify the use of the original material with the phrase *as cited in* (not italicized). Provide an entry for the secondary source you used in the reference list.

Staddon, J. E. (2001). *Adaptive dynamics: The theoretical analysis of behavior.* Cambridge: Massachusetts Institute of Technology Press.

Collier presents a somewhat unusual schema related to the "feeding strategies" of rats (as cited in Staddon, 2001).

Audiovisual sources—films, recordings, speeches, works of art, and other visual images—are not used frequently in APA papers. Nevertheless, they can provide interesting support for discussions and create variety within a paper.

To cite an audiovisual source in a reference list, follow the guidelines in this chapter.

7a   A Film

An entry for a film begins with the producer's or director's name (with the word *Producer* or *Director* in parentheses but not italicized), followed by the year of the film's release, the film title (italicized), and a descriptive title (in brackets). The entry ends with the country of origin and the company.

Include other people's contributions after the film title (in brackets), using brief phrases (*Narr. by, With, Written by*—not italicized) to clarify their roles.

Pollack, S. (Director). (1985). *Out of Africa* [Film]. United
    States: Universal.

> ***In-text citation***   (Pollack, 1985)

Fincher, D. (Director). (1999). *Fight club* [Film]. [With Brad
Pitt, Edward Norton, & Helena Bonham Carter].
United States: Regency-20th Century Fox.

> *In-text citation*   (Fincher, 1999)

Note that a dual-release film requires the names of both
the independent studio and the major distributor (the
large film studio). The names are joined by a hyphen,
without spaces.

7b   A Filmstrip or Slide Program

A filmstrip or slide program is cited just as a film is, with
one exception: Include a descriptive title such as *Filmstrip* in brackets (but not italicized) after the title.

Songs of the Civil War: Filmstrip 6 [Filmstrip with audiotape].
(1965). *Our heritage of American music.* United States:
Society for Visual Education.

> *In-text citation*   (*Songs of the Civil War,* 1965) or (*Songs,*
> 1965)

Note that one filmstrip from a collection is presented in the
same pattern as one book from a multivolume collection.

Washington, D.C. [Slides]. (1953). United States: Inter-
American Features.

> *In-text citation*   (*Washington, D.C.,* 1953)

7c   A Television Broadcast

A regular television program is listed by producer or
director, broadcast date when appropriate, the title (italicized), a descriptive phrase (in brackets), the city (and state
or country, if necessary), and the network (spelled out
completely). Include other people's contributions after the
program title (in brackets), using brief phrases (*Narr. by,
With, Written by*—not italicized) to clarify their roles.

Burrows, J. (Director.) (2000). *Will and Grace* [Television
series]. [With Eric McCormack, Debra Messing,
Sean Hayes, & Megan Mullally]. New York: National
Broadcasting Company.

> *In-text citation*   (Burrows, 2000)

To refer to an individual episode, insert its title after the specific broadcast date, without special punctuation; add a descriptive phrase in brackets. Then, use the word *In* (not italicized) to introduce the program title. The rest of the entry follows normal patterns.

Crichton, M. (Producer). (1995, February 23). Sleepless in Chicago [Television series episode]. In *ER*. New York: National Broadcasting Company.

> *In-text citation* (Crichton, 1995)

7d   A Radio Broadcast

An entry for a radio broadcast follows the guidelines for a television broadcast, although in some instances a broadcast will not have an assigned title.

Murrow, E. R. (1940, September 13). [Radio broadcast]. New York: WCBS.

> *In-text citation* (Murrow, 1940)

7e   A Recording

An entry for a recording begins with the writer-composer's name, the date of the recording, and the selection title. If the recording artist is not the writer-composer, place his or her name in brackets, using the phrase *Recorded by* (not italicized). Then, include the album title (introduced by the word *On*, not italicized), the recording format (in brackets), the city (and state or country, if necessary), and company.

If the recording contains previously recorded material, include information about original recordings in parentheses at the end.

The Beatles. (2000). *1* [CD]. Hollywood, CA: Apple-Capital. (Original work recorded 1962–1970)

> *In-text citation* (The Beatles, 2000)

This entry indicates that materials recorded in 1962–1970 were, in this case, re-released in 2000.

To emphasize a single selection on a recording, include the title of the brief work (without special punctuation), followed by the title of the complete recording and other production information.

Jagger, M., & Richards, K. (1986). You can't always get what you want [Recorded by The Rolling Stones]. On *Hot rocks: 1964–1971* [CD]. New York: Abkco. (Original work recorded in 1969)

In-text citation (Jagger & Richards, 1986)

7f An Interview

An interview is considered a personal communication. As such, it is not included in a reference list. However, it is cited in the text of the paper by enclosing the phrase *personal communication* (not italicized) and the date in parentheses.

J. Kalb (personal communication, April 4, 2002) stressed the importance of double-blind studies.

7g A Transcript

A transcript of a program is presented according to the source of the original broadcast, with clarifying information provided in brackets. The entry ends with information about availability.

Hackney, S., Alberta, A., & Burns, W. (1995, March 2). National Endowment for the Humanities faces cuts. *All things considered* [Radio broadcast]. [Transcript]. Washington, DC: National Public Radio. Available: Journal Graphics On-line.

In-text citation (Hackney, Alberta, & Burns, 1995)

Watkins, T., Stark, L., Kennedy, W., & Pelley, S. (1995, April 28). McVeigh said to have mentioned other bombings in letter. [Transcript]. *Daybreak* [Television broadcast]. Atlanta, GA: Cable News Network. Available: Journal Graphics On-line.

In-text citation (Watkins, Stark, Kennedy, & Pelley, 1995)

7h A Lecture or Speech

An entry for a lecture or speech includes the speaker's name, the date of the speech, the title of the speech (italicized) or a description of it (in brackets), a series title or a description of the speech-making context, and the location (most often, the city and state).

Gould, S. J. (1998, November 4). *Interactions of art and science and the largely arbitrary nature of academic boundaries.* Lecture presented for the Stanford Presidential Lectures in Humanities and Arts, Stanford University, Stanford, CA.

> *In-text citation*   (Gould, 1998)

Nixon, R. (1974, August 8). [Resignation speech]. Speech presented at the White House, Washington, DC.

> *In-text citation*   (Nixon, 1974)

Note that *Resignation speech,* the descriptive title of the speech, is given within brackets and is not italicized.

7i   A Work of Art

An entry for a work of art includes the name of the artist when known, the completion date, the title of the work (either assigned by the artist or attributed to the work), a description of the medium (enclosed in brackets), the museum or collection name, and the city (and state, province, or country, if necessary). Note that when artists assign titles, they are italicized; however, do not italicize titles that other people have assigned to the work.

Gauguin, P. (1891). *The brooding woman* [Painting in oil]. Worcester Art Museum, Worcester, MA.

> *In-text citation*   (Gauguin, 1891)

Amateis, E. R. (1958). Jonas Edward Salk [Sculpture in bronze]. National Portrait Gallery, Washington, DC.

> *In-text citation*   (Amateis, 1958)

Amateis, the artist, did not formally title this sculpture. "Jonas Edward Salk" is the attributed title of the statue and, therefore, is not italicized.

7j   A Map, Graph, Table, or Chart

A map, graph, table, or chart is treated like a book. Include the name of the author (if known), artist, designer, scientist, or other person—or group—responsible for the map, graph, table, or chart. It is followed by the publication date, in parentheses. Include the title as it is presented in the source, but without special punctuation such as quotation marks. Follow the title with a descriptive label in brackets, followed by a period. Then include whatever entry information is required for the source.

Engel, B. S. (1990). Descriptive literacy inventory [Chart]. From An approach to assessment in early literacy. In C. Kamii (Ed.), *Achievement testing in the early grades: The games grown-ups play* (p. 128). Washington, DC: National Association for the Education of Young Children.

   In-text citation   (Engel, 1990)

Kane, T. J. (1999). Distribution of federal loans to college undergraduates [Chart]. In T. J. Kane, *The price of admission: Rethinking how Americans pay for college* (p. 94). Washington, DC: Brookings Institute.

   In-text citation   (Kane, 1999)

7k A Cartoon

Begin with the cartoonist's name, the date on which the cartoon appeared, the title of the cartoon (if there is one), and the word *Cartoon* in brackets, but not italicized. Then include the entry information required for the source.

Davis, J., & Hart, S. (1991, January). Groan with the wind [Cartoon]. *Mad*, 42–47.

   In-text citation   (Davis & Hart, 1991)

Mad magazine does not use volume numbers, so none is included in the entry.

Stein, E. (2001, January 5). Okay, okay, Greenspan, I'm impressed. But I still want a tax cut [Cartoon]. *USA Today*, p. A13.

   In-text citation   (Stein, 2001)

8 Citing Electronic Sources

Electronic sources exist in many formats—online databases, electronic publications of traditional print sources, organizational Web sites, CD-ROMs, e-mail –based discussion groups, and others. To allow researchers to cite these sources, APA has developed the relatively simple and flexible strategy of, first, following entry patterns that exist for comparable print sources and, second, adding information about electronic access. With this system, the entry ends with what APA calls a "retrieval statement." For online sources, today's most common source, the retrieval statement follows this pattern:

Retrieved *Month, day, year,* from *electronic address*

Notice that the retrieval statement has no ending punctuation, because a closing period might be misconstrued as part of the electronic address.

As you gather entry information to cite electronic sources, you must be resourceful to find important information. Your goal should be to gather the most complete set of information possible for each electronic source, following the guidelines in this chapter.

8a An Online Scholarly Project, Information Database, or Professional Web Site

If you refer to an entire online scholarly project, information database, or professional Web site, you do not need to include an entry in your reference list. However, you must identify the title of the source clearly in the text of your paper (capitalized but without special punctuation) and provide a very basic in-text entry (the electronic address), as in these samples:

> The Victorian Web presents a wide range of information on the period, ranging from discussions of art to important people, from the history of ideas to the elements of popular culture (http://landow.stg. brown.edu/ victorian/victor.html).

> The UNICEF Web site provides links to a variety of useful sources that discuss the welfare of children around the world (http://www.unicef.org/).

8b A Source from an Online Scholarly Project, Information Database, or Professional Web Site

To cite a source—an article, illustration, map, or other element—from an online scholarly project, information database, or professional Web site, include (1) the name of the author (or artist, compiler, or editor) of the individual source, if available; (2) the posting or revision date; (3) the title of the source, without special punctuation; (4) the name of the project, database, or Web site; and (5) the retrieval statement.

Cody, D. (2000). Queen Victoria. The Victorian Web. Retrieved
    January 19, 2002, from http://landow.stg.brown.
    edu/victorian/victor6.html

>   ***In-text citation***   (Cody, 2000)

Expenditures for health care plans by employers and
    employees. (1998, December 7). Washington, DC:
    Bureau of Labor Statistics. Retrieved February 17,
    2002, from http://stats.bls.gov/

>   ***In-text citation***   ("Expenditures for Health Care Plans,"
>   1998) or ("Expenditures," 1998)

8c   An Article in an Online Journal

At present, articles in online journals fall into three categories: (1) articles that reproduce printed articles without
any changes, (2) articles that reproduce printed articles
but include additional information or appear in a different form, and (3) articles that are available only in electronic form. Three forms of reference-list entries allow
writers to document these patterns clearly.

If an online journal article presents an exact version of
a print article, prepare a standard journal entry (see
chapter 5, "An Article in a Journal with Continuous
Paging" and "An Article in a Journal with Separate Paging"). However, after the article title, insert the phrase
Electronic version, not italicized, in brackets.

Marriott, L. K., Hauss-Wegzyniak, B., Benton, R. S.,
    Vraniak, P. D., & Wenk, G. L. (2002). Long-term
    estrogen therapy worsens the behavioral and
    neuropathological consequences of chronic brain
    inflammation [Electronic version]. *Behavioral
    Neuroscience, 116*, 902–911.

>   ***First in-text citation***   (Marriott, Hauss-Wegzyniak, Ben-
>   ton, Vraniak, & Wenk, 2002).

>   ***Second and subsequent citations***   (Marriott et al., 2002)

If an online journal article presents a print article with
additional material or in different form, prepare a complete entry for the print form (see chapter 5, "An Article
in a Journal with Continuous Paging" and "An Article in
a Journal with Separate Paging"). At the end of the entry,
add a retrieval statement.

Parrot, A. C. (1999). Does cigarette smoking *cause* stress? *American Psychologist, 54,* 817–820. Retrieved May 10, 2002, from http://www.apa.org/journals/amp/ amp5410817.html

   In-text citation   (Parrot, 1999)

If a journal article appears only in online form, provide (1) the name of the author, if appropriate; (2) the date in parentheses; (3) the title of the article; (4) the name of the journal and the volume number, italicized, and the issue number (if needed) in parentheses, not italicized; and (5) the retrieval statement.

Indick, W. (2000). Gender differences in moral judgment: Is non-consequential reasoning a factor? *Current Research in Social Psychology, 5*(2). Retrieved November 11, 2002, from http://www.uiowa.edu/ ~grpproc/crisp/crisp5.2.htm

   In-text citation   (Indick, 2000)

8d   An Article in an Online Magazine

To cite an article in an online magazine, provide (1) the name of the author, if appropriate; (2) the date in parentheses; (3) the title of the article; (4) the name of the magazine and volume number, italicized; and (5) the retrieval statement.

Begley, S., & Brant, M. (1999, February 15). The real scandal. *Newsweek, 135.* Retrieved February 16, 2002, from http://www.newsweek.com/nw=srv/printed/int/ socu/sp0107_7.htm

   In-text citation   (Begley & Brant, 1999)

Wheelright, J. (2001, January). Betting on designer genes. *Smithsonian, 31.* Retrieved January 18, 2002, from http://www.smithsonianmag.sr.edu/smithsonian/ issues01/jan01/gene.html

   In-text citation   (Wheelright, 2001)

8e   An Article in an Online Newspaper

To cite an article in an online newspaper, provide (1) the name of the author, if appropriate; (2) the date of publication in parentheses; (3) the title of the article; (4) the name of the newspaper, italicized; and (5) the retrieval statement.

Rodriguez, C. (2001, January 9). Amid dispute, plight of illegal workers revisited. *Boston Globe*. Retrieved January 10, 2002, from http://www.boston.com/dailyglobe2/010/ nation/Amid_dispute_plight_of_illegal_workers_ revisited+.shtml

> ***In-text citation***   (Rodriguez, 2001)

TWA agrees to buyout by American Airlines. (2001, January 10). *Los Angeles Times*. Retrieved January 10, 2002, from http://www.latimes.com/business/ updates/ap_amair010110.htm

> ***In-text citation***   ("TWA Agrees to Buyout by American Airlines," 2001) or ("TWA," 2001)

8f   An Article in an Online Newsletter

An entry for an online newsletter follows the same pattern as that for an online newspaper, except that it includes the volume and issue number if they are provided.

Light, T. (2002, May). Canadian tobacco tax measures. *Alcohol & Tobacco Newsletter, 2*(5). Retrieved July 27, 2002, from http://www.atf.treas.gov/alcohol

> ***In-text citation***   (Light, 2002)

8g   An Online Book

Online books exist in two forms: those previously published and now available electronically and those available only in electronic form.

To cite an online book that has a corresponding print version, first prepare a standard entry describing the print version (see chapter 6). Then provide the retrieval statement, which includes (1) the date you accessed the site; (2) the name of the source, whether online project, database, or Web site; and (3) the general electronic address of the site where the book can be retrieved, rather than the specific electronic address for the book.

Lofting, H. (1922). *The voyages of Doctor Dolittle.*
Philadelphia: Lippincott. Retrieved February 2, 2002,
from Project Gutenberg: ftp://ibiblio.org/pub/docs/
books/-gutenberg/

In-text citation (Lofting, 1922)

To cite an online book that is available only in electronic form, provide (1) the name of the author or
editor; (2) the date in parentheses; (3) the title, italicized; and (4) the retrieval statement.

Buxhoeveden, S. (n.d.). *The life and tragedy of Alexandra
Feodorvna, empress of Russia.* Retrieved January 15,
2002, from the Russian History Web site: http://www.
alexanderpalace.org

In-text citation (Buxhoeveden, n.d.)

8h An Article in an Online Encyclopedia or Other Reference Work

To cite an article from an online encyclopedia or reference
work, provide (1) the author of the entry, if there is one;
(2) the date, in parentheses; (3) the title of the entry exactly
as it appears in the source, without special punctuation;
(4) the name of the reference work, italicized; (5) facts of
publication, if the source first existed in print form; and
(6) the retrieval statement.

Children in foster care. (2000). [Chart]. *Infoplease almanac.*
Retrieved January 13, 2002, from http://www.
infoplease.com/

In-text citation ("Children in Foster Care," 2000)

Machismo. (2000). *Yourdictionary.* Retrieved March 27, 2002,
from http://www.yourdictionary.com/

In-text citation ("Machismo," 2000)

8i An Online Government Document

To citc an online version of a government document—
a book, report, proceedings, brochure, or other source—
first provide the information required for the print source
(see chapter 6, "A Government Document—Committee,

Commission, Department"). Then continue the entry with the retrieval statement.

Labs, E. J. (2000, October). *Budgeting for naval forces: Structuring tomorrow's Navy at today's funding level.* Washington, DC: Government Printing Office. Retrieved May 6, 2002, from http://www.cbo.gov/

　　In-text citation　(Labs, 2000)

Kreider, H., Mayer, E., & Vaughn, P. (2000). *Early childhood digest: Helping parents communicate better with schools.* Retrieved March 19, 2002, from http://www.ed.gov/

　　In-text citation　(Kreider, Mayer, & Vaughn, 2000)

8j　An Online Transcript of a Lecture or Speech

To cite an online transcript of a lecture or speech, first provide the information required for a lecture or a speech (see chapter 7, "A Lecture or Speech"). Then include (1) the word *Transcript,* not italicized and in brackets, and (2) the retrieval statement.

Bush, G. W. (2000, September 6). [Address]. Address presented at the American Legion Convention. Annual Meeting, Milwaukee, WI. [Transcript]. Retrieved December 23, 2002, from http://www.georgewbush.com/news/speeches/090600_legion.html

　　In-text citation　(Bush, 2000)

King, M. L., Jr. (1964, December 10). Nobel Peace Prize acceptance speech. Nobel Prize Ceremony, Oslo, Sweden. [Transcript]. Retrieved January 31, 2002, from http://www.stanford.edu/group/king

　　In-text citation　(King, 1964)

8k　An Online Map, Graph, Table, or Chart

To cite an online map, graph, table, or chart, first provide the information required for the kind of visual element (see chapter 7, "A Map, Graph, Table, or Chart"). Then provide the retrieval statement.

United States Geological Survey. (2001, February 16).
Alcatraz Island [Map]. Encarta. Retrieved February 16,
2002, from http://www.terraserver.microsoft.com/
image.asp?S=14&T+2&X=172&Y=1308&Z=10&W=0

In-text citation   (United States Geological Survey, 2001)

United States Census Bureau. (2000, September 26). Poverty
rates by age [Graph]. *Poverty in the United States: 1999.*
Retrieved March 20, 2002, from http://www.census.gov/
hhes/poverty/poverty99/povage99.html

In-text citation   (United States Census Bureau, 2000)

8l   An Online Transcript of a Television or Radio Broadcast

To cite an online transcript of a television or radio
broadcast, first provide the information required for the
audiovisual entry (see chapter 7, "A Television Broadcast"
or "A Radio Broadcast"). Then include (1) the word *Transcript,* in brackets but not italicized, and (2) the retrieval
statement.

High drama in the high court. (2001, December 1). *Nightline*
[Television broadcast]. [With Ted Koppel]. New York:
American Broadcasting Company. [Transcript]. Retrieved January 11, 2002, from http://abcnews.go.com/
onair/nightline/transcripts/ nl001201_trans.html

In-text citation   ("High Drama in the High Court," 2001)

Aldrin, B. (1998, July 16). [Interview]. *Weekend edition—
Sunday* [Radio broadcast]. Washington, DC: National
Public Radio. [Transcript]. Retrieved May 6, 2002, from
http://www.hq.nasa.gov/alsj/frame.html

In-text citation   (Aldrin, 1998)

8m   A CD-ROM Source

Although CD-ROMs are being phased out in most libraries,
you may still need to cite a CD-ROM source.

If a CD-ROM source reproduces material available in
print form, begin the entry with full print information:
author (or editor), date, title, and facts of publication (see

chapters 5–7 for complete patterns for entries); then add a retrieval statement. If the material is not available in print form, begin the entry with identifying information: (1) author, if given; (2) date; (3) title, italicized; and (4) the retrieval statement.

The retrieval statement for a CD-ROM source includes (1) the title of the source, without special punctuation, and (2) in parentheses, the name of the database; the word *CD-ROM,* not italicized; the release date; and an item number, if applicable.

> On the brink: An interview with Yitzhak Rabin. (1994, April 23). *Jerusalem Post, 16.* Retrieved from PAIS International (Silverplatter, CD-ROM, 1995 release).
>
> ***In-text citation*** ("On the Brink," 1994)

> Welmers, W. E. (1994). African languages. *The New Grolier Multimedia Encyclopedia.* Retrieved from Grolier database (Grolier, CD-ROM, 1994 release).
>
> ***In-text citation*** (Welmers, 1994)

8n An E-mail Interview

An interview conducted through e-mail correspondence is considered personal communication. As such, it is not included in the reference list. However, it is cited in the text of the paper by enclosing the phrase *personal communication* (not italicized) and the date of the e-mail in parentheses.

> H. S. Davis (personal communication, March 13, 2002) noted that classroom technology is only as good as the people who use it.

8o An Online Posting

To cite an online posting to a forum or discussion group, provide (1) the name of the author, if known; (2) the official or descriptive title of the posting; (3) the phrase *Message posted to,* not italicized; (4) the name of the forum or discussion group, followed by a comma; (5) the phrase *archived at,* not italicized; and (6) the URL.

Hamel, E. (2000, November 13). Invasive species information source. Message posted to Meadows and Prairies Forum, archived at http://forums.gardenweb/load/natives/msg112040189632.html?15

In-text citation   (Hamel, 2000)

Whinney, K. (2001, January 11). Discussion of *A clockwork orange*. Message posted to Book Lovers' Discussion, archived at http://www.Whatamigoingtoread.com/book.asp?bookid=6395

In-text citation   (Whinney, 2001)

Running head: BEYOND BIRTH ORDER

A working title, followed by 5 spaces and the page number, appears ½ inch from the top of every page.

The running head, labeled, is in capitals. The label starts at the left margin, 2 lines below the header.

Beyond Birth Order:

Recognizing Other Variables

Elissa Allen and Jeremy Reynolds

Psychology 256

Identifying information is centered from top to bottom and from left to right.

Abstract

Although scholars continue to make a case for birth-order effects in children's development, exclusive reliance on this useful but one-dimensional criterion ignores other variables that affect children's personal, intellectual, and social development. The sex of other siblings, the time between births, the size of the family, the age of the mother, the psychological condition of the children, the absence of a parent, and the birth order of the parents also influence a child's development.

The running head is ½ inch from the top of the page.

The label has normal capitalization.

The paragraph is not indented.

The abstract (no more than 120 words) describes the paper.

Beyond Birth Order:

Recognizing Other Variables

The paper begins on page 3.

The title, centered, has normal capitalization.

The use of allusions (an introductory strategy) creates interest.

Historical context established

Sigmund Freud, Queen Elizabeth II, Albert Einstein, William Shakespeare, George Washington, Jacqueline Kennedy, John Milton, Julius Caesar, Leontyne Price, and Winston Churchill. What do these famous people have in common? They were all first-born children. The fact that so many important people in all spheres of influence have been first-born children has lent credence to the notion that birth order helps determine the kind of people we become.

Note the use of past tense to discuss scholarship.

General references cite author and date.

Scientific studies over the years have, in fact, suggested that birth order affects an individual's development. For example, recent studies (Pine, 1995) have suggested that first-born children acquire language skills sooner than later-born children. The Parent and Child Guidance Center (2001) explained this premise very simply: "Because they spend so much time with adults, [first-born children] talk in more of an adult way." Further, Ernst and Angst (1983) explained the underlying premise of birth order effects this way: "Everybody agrees that birth-order differences must arise from differential socialization by the parents. There is, however, no general theory on how this differential socialization actually works" (p. x). Stein (2001) adds that birth-order effects are more pronounced in families that are competitive and democratic. It is not surprising, then, that a general theory has not emerged because many other variables besides birth order influence an individual's personal, intellectual, and social development.

Specific references cite author and date, as well as specific page.

Thesis statement

Beyond Birth Order   4

Sex of the Siblings

While acknowledging that birth order plays a part in an individual's development, scholars have begun to recognize that it is only one variable. For example, Sutton-Smith and Rosenberg (1970) observed that even in two-child families there are four possible variations for sibling relationships based on gender: (1) first-born female, second-born female; (2) first-born female, second-born male; (3) first-born male, second-born male; (4) first-born male, second-born female. In families with three children, the variations increase to 24. To suggest that being the first-born child is the same in all of these contexts ignores too many variables.

Time Between Births

Forer (1976) suggested that when the births of children are separated by five or more years, the effects of birth order are changed. For example, in a family with four children (with children aged 12, 6, 4, and 2 years old), the second child would be more likely to exhibit the characteristics of an oldest child because of his or her nearness in age to the younger children and the six-year separation in age from the oldest child. The pattern would differ from that of a sibling in a four-child family if the children were spaced fewer than three years apart (for example, if the children were 10, 8, 5, and 3 years old); this second child would exhibit the characteristics typical of a second-middle child.

Size of Family

Studies have also suggested that the size of the family modifies the effects of birth order. Whereas in a moderate-sized family (two to four children) the

Headings divide the discussion into subtopics.

Note the use of a list with numbered elements.

Common knowledge suggests that the number increases to 24.

A summary presents Forer's ideas clearly.

Numbers used in comparisons must all appear in the same form.

Elissa and Jeremy provide their own example; it does not require documentation.

first-born child usually achieves the highest level of

Scholars are always referred to by last names only.

education, Forer (1969) observed that "a first-born child from a large family has often been found to obtain less education than a last-born child from such a family" (p. 24). Whether this occurs because large families tend to have lower socioeconomic status or whether it is the result of varied family dynamics, the overall size of the family seems to alter the preconceived notions of birth order and its influence on a child's development.

Age of the Mother

Studies have suggested that a mother's age has a strong bearing on the child's learned behavior, regardless of birth order. Sutton-Smith and Rosenberg (1970) offered this perspective:

Long quotations are indented 5 spaces and double-spaced.

The parenthetical note follows the closing period of a set-in quotation.

On a more obvious level, younger mothers have more stamina and vigor than older mothers. One speculation in the literature is that they are also more anxious and uncertain about their child-training procedures, and that this has an effect of inducing anxiety in their offspring. (p. 138)

It seems safe to assume, then, that the third child of a woman of 28 will have a different experience growing up than the third child of a woman of 39. They may share the same relational patterns with their siblings, but they will not share the same patterns with their mothers.

Psychological Factors

Early studies on birth order failed to account for psychological differences among children, even among those who shared the same birth status. Forer (1969) asserted, however, that "special conditions involving a child in a family may change the birth-order effect both for him and his siblings" (p. 19).

Beyond Birth Order   6

Such conditions as a child's mental retardation, severe hearing loss, blindness, disabling handicaps — or even extreme beauty, exceptional intelligence, or great physical skill — can alter the dynamics of the family and consequently affect the traditionally described effects of birth order. In short, a middle child whose physiological conditions are outside the normal spectrum — because of different potential and opportunity — will not have the same life experiences as a middle child who is considered average.

A summary usefully connects ideas.

Absence of a Parent

Parents may be absent from family units for a variety of reasons: a parent may die, creating a permanent void in a family unit; a parent may be gone to war or be hospitalized for an extended period, creating a temporary but notable disruption in the family; or a parent may travel for business or be gone for brief periods to attend school, creating a brief but obvious interruption in the family's normal workings. These conditions affect a child's experiences and can, under certain circumstances, mitigate the effects of birth order. Toman (1993) explained that the effects will be greater

a. The more recently they have occurred,

b. The earlier in a person's life they have occurred,

c. The older the person lost is (in relation to the oldest family member),

d. The longer the person has lived together with the lost person,

e. The smaller the family,

f. The greater the imbalance of the sexes in the family resulting from the loss,

g. The longer it takes the family to find a replacement for the lost person,

A long quoted list must represent the original source as accurately as possible.

 h. The greater the number of losses, and the graver
   the losses, that have occurred before. (pp. 41–42)

Such disruptions—whether major or minor—alter the
family unit and often have a greater influence on the
children than the traditional effects of birth order.

Birth Order of Parents

 A number of scholars have asserted that the birth
order of parents influences to a high degree their inter-
relationships with their children and, consequently,
creates an impact that extends beyond the simple birth
order of the children. Toman (1993) described the
family relationships, based on birth order, that promise
the least conflict and, hence, best situation for
children's development:

> If the mother is the youngest sister of
> a brother and has an older son and a younger
> daughter, she can identify with her daughter
> and the daughter with the mother. The daugh-
> ter, too, is the younger sister of a brother.
> Moreover, the mother has no trouble dealing
> with her son, for she had an older brother in
> her original family and her son, too, is an
> older brother of a sister. (p. 199)

Toman's assumption that parents relate better to their
children when they have shared similar sibling-related
experiences leads to this assumption: When parents
can create a positive and productive home
environment (because of familiar familial relationships), the children will benefit. When conflict occurs
because sibling relations are unfamiliar, everyone
suffers. Parent-child relationships—determined, at
least in part, by the parents' own birth orders—would

Beyond Birth Order   8

consequently vary from family to family, even when children of those families share the same birth order.

Conclusion

According to U.S. Census information, collected from 92,119 randomly selected mothers, 28% of children are first born, 28% second born, 20% middle born, and 18% youngest born (Simpson, Bloom, Newlon, & Arminio, 1994). As long as census takers, scholars, family members, parents, and children think in terms of birth order, we will have an oversimplified perspective of why children develop as they do. Yet recent studies (Parish, 1990) have suggested that adolescents recognize that family structure and personal interaction have a stronger bearing on their perceptions of themselves, other family members, and their families than do birth order or even gender. And, importantly, Web sites such as Matthias Romppel's Birth Order Research approach the issue cautiously, suggesting that birth-order effects on children are changeable (http://www.romppel.de/birth-order/). Perhaps we should take our cues from these young people and current scholars and recognize that birth order is but one interesting variable in personality development.

Percentages are represented in numeral-symbol form.

Multiple authors are listed, with an ampersand between the last names.

A reference to a complete Web site occurs in the paper but does not appear in the reference list.

Page numbers continue sequentially.

The descriptive title is centered.

Names are repeated in subsequent citations.

Note that italics are used, not underlining.

Note: First lines are at the normal margin; subsequent lines are indented.

References

Birth order and your child. (2001). Parent and Child Guidance Center. Retrieved March 11, 2002, from http://trfn.clpgh.org/pcgc/birthorder.html

Ernst, C., & Angst, J. (1983). *Birth order: Its influence on personality.* Berlin: Springer.

Forer, L. K. (1969). *Birth order and life roles.* Springfield, IL: Thomas.

Forer, L. K. (1976). *The birth order factor: How your personality is influenced by your place in the family.* New York: McKay.

Parish, T. S. (1990). Evaluations of family by youth: Do they vary as a function of family structure, gender, and birth order? *Adolescence, 25,* 353–356.

Pine, J. M. (1995). Variations in vocabulary development as a function of birth order. *Child Development, 66,* 272–281.

Simpson, P. W., Bloom, J. W., Newlon, B. J., & Arminio, L. (1994). Birth-order proportions of the general population in the United States. *Individual Psychology: Journal of Alderian Theory, 50,* 173–182.

Stein, H. T. (2001). Alderian overview of birth order characteristics. Alfred Alder Institute of San Francisco. Retrieved March 6, 2002, from http://ourworld.compuserve.com/homepages/hstein/birthord.htm

Sutton-Smith, B., & Rosenberg, B. G. (1970). *The sibling.* New York: Holt.

Toman, W. (1993). *Family constellation: Its effects on personality and social behavior.* New York: Springer.

Running head: TEST QUESTIONS

The running head, labeled, is in capitals (2 lines below the page header).

A Piece in the Test-Anxiety Puzzle:

Students' Reactions to Kinds of Test Questions

Gabriel Stevenson

Educational Psychology 310

Identifying information is centered from top to bottom and left to right.

Abstract

The purpose of this brief study was to determine whether specific kinds of questions produced anxiety in students. The results of a survey of 89 high school freshmen indicate that true/false, multiple-choice, and matching are low-anxiety question formats, whereas essay, fill-in-the-blank, and listing are high-anxiety question formats. However, the study revealed that students' anxiety levels related to question types do not vary dramatically, either by question type or by students' performance levels, as indicated by previous grades.

The label has normal capitalization.

The paragraph is not indented.

The abstract (no more than 120 words) describes the paper.

A Piece in the Test-Anxiety Puzzle:

Students' Reactions to Kinds of Test Questions

Today's students are faced with an increasing number of tests. Not only do they take tests for their individual classes, but they also take state-mandated competency tests to progress through school and standardized achievement tests to gain admission to colleges and universities. With the emphasis currently being placed on tests, it is no wonder that many students are now experiencing test anxiety.

One area, however, has not received sufficient attention: students' reactions to specific kinds of test questions. Consequently, using data collected from a sampling of high school students, this brief study attempts to discover with what types of test questions students are most comfortable and what kinds of questioning techniques produce the greatest amount of insecurity or anxiety.

Literature Review

The nature of students' test anxiety has been—and continues to be—studied by scholars in education, psychology, and related fields. By understanding the forms, causes, and results of test anxiety, they hope to provide the means for students and educators to address the problem in helpful ways.

Spielberger and Vagg (1995) have discussed testing in a large cultural context, cataloguing the ever-increasing number of tests used in educational and work-related settings. Wigfield and Eccles (1989) have described the nature of test anxiety, providing useful categories and explanations to enhance the understanding of this multifaceted problem. Hancock (2001) has further contextualized the testing situation

---

The paper begins on page 3.

The title, centered, has normal capitalization.

An unlabeled introduction establishes the context for the paper and clarifies the topic.

Level-1 headings divide the discussion into major subtopics.

The "Literature Review" summarizes the scholarship on the topic.

Test Questions   4

by describing the high-stakes environments in which tests are given.

Other scholars have explored the cognitive processes that are related to test anxiety. Schutz, Davis, and Schwanenflugel (2002) have distinguished between high and low levels of test anxiety and have discussed the ways students perceive the test-taking process and the ways they cope. Others have addressed students' self-awareness about the emotional nature of the testing process and their own procedures for handling emotion during testing (Weiner 1994; Zeidner 1995a, 1995b).

References to scholars correspond to entries in the reference list.

Multiple references are separated by semicolons.

Yet other scholars have discussed test anxiety among special student populations. Swanson and Howell (1996) have expressed particular concern that test anxiety among disabled students can lead to poor test performance, which in turn can lead to poor overall academic performance and low self-esteem. Further, Nelson, Jayanthi, Epstein, and Bursuck (2000) have presented information on alternatives to and adaptations of traditional testing that can allow special-needs students to demonstrate what they know without the additional burden of test anxiety.

These studies have laid a contextual groundwork for further study, especially in areas such as test design and test preparation.

Method

Participants

The survey group was composed of 89 high school freshmen (44 females and 45 males) from three classes. The students were enrolled in a required (and untracked) freshman English class that included students of varied abilities at a consolidated high school in west-central

"Method" subsections (using level-3 headings) describe various facets of the study.

Indiana. The students had completed one grading period; their grades ranged from *A* to *F*.

Materials

An in-text reference directs readers to figure that follows the paper.

Students were given a brief questionnaire (see Figure 1) that included these elements: (1) an element to determine gender, (2) an element to record their grades in English during the previous nine weeks, (3) a six-element questionnaire using a Likert-type scale so that students could indicate their anxiety-related responses to six types of test questions, and (4) a section for additional comments about types of test questions.

Procedures

Materials and procedures are briefly described.

The students' teacher distributed the questionnaire at the beginning of each of the three class periods and read the instructions aloud, emphasizing that students were to respond to the types of questions based on their entire testing experiences, not just those with English tests. Students were then given ten minutes to complete the questionnaire; most completed the questionnaires in fewer than five minutes.

Results

The "Results" section summarizes the data.

The most general analysis of the data involved computing students' ratings of question types using the Likert-type scale (1=*secure,* 3–4=*no reaction,* 6=*insecure*). Percentages of students' responses appear in Table 1.

Low-Anxiety Question Types

Subsections (using level-3 headings) divide the summary into useful categories.

The findings indicate that true/false test questions create the least anxiety, with 31.4% of students giving it a 1 rating; in addition, 81.9% rated true/false as a 1, 2, or 3, indicating little anxiety. Matching and multiple-choice questions also achieved low anxiety ratings, with 25.8% of students giving them a 1 rating; 79.7% rated matching as a 1, 2, or 3, indicating little anxiety. Interestingly, 84.3% rated multiple-choice questions as a 1, 2, or 3, making it the question type that produces the least anxiety in the greatest percentage of students.

High-Anxiety Question Types

The findings indicate that essay questions create the most anxiety, with 49.4% of students giving them a 6 rating; further, 71.9% rated essay questions as a 4, 5, or 6, indicating a high degree of anxiety. Fill-in-the-blank questions also achieved a high-anxiety rating, with 24.6% of students giving them a 6 rating; 65.1% rated fill-in-the-blank questions as a 4, 5, or 6, indicating a high degree of anxiety. Finally, 21.4% of students rated listing questions as a 6; 65.3% rated them as a 4, 5, or 6, making this a high-stress question type.

> The summary must correlate with the information included in figures or tables.

Mean Responses

The mean responses to the question types (1 = *secure;* 3–4 = *no reaction;* 6 = *insecure*) correlate with the individual low-anxiety and high-anxiety ratings given by students, as shown in Table 2. True/false (2.35), multiple-choice (2.43), and matching (2.53) remain in the low-anxiety category, but multiple-choice and matching reverse their rating order. Essay (4.56), fill-in-the-blank (4.27), and listing (4.16) remain in the high-anxiety category; they retain the same rating order.

> Tables are numbered sequentially; they are presented after the paper.

Mean responses by students' grade categories show slightly varied preferences among high-performing and low-performing students: *A* students (1: matching; 2: multiple-choice; 3: true/false; 4: fill-in-the-blank; 5–6: listing and essay), *B* students (1: multiple-choice; 2: matching; 3: true/false; 4: listing; 5–6: fill-in-the-blank and essay), *C* students (1: matching; 2: multiple-choice; 3: true/false; 4–5: fill-in-the-blank and listing; 6: essay),

D students (1: true/false; 2: multiple-choice; 3: matching; 4: listing; 5: fill-in-the-blank; 6: essay), and *F* students (1: true/false; 2: multiple-choice; 3: matching; 4: listing; 5: fill-in-the-blank; 6: essay).

An average of the mean responses to all six question types for each grade category indicates an increasing degree of anxiety: for *A* students, the averaged mean response is 2.75; for *B* students, 3.08; for *C* students, 3.57; for *D* students, 3.61; and for *F* students, 3.83. Although the increments are small, there is a steady progression from one student group to the next; however, none of the averaged means falls far from the 3–4 range *(no reaction),* suggesting that, generally, no question format makes students as a group feel either very secure or very anxious.

The "Discussion" section provides commentary on the data, noting the data's correlation with the hypothesis.

Discussion

The data indicate that, for students, question types fall into two distinct groups: low-stress questions (true/false, multiple-choice, matching) and high-stress questions (listing, fill-in-the-blank, essay). However, the data also indicate that, on average, students' anxiety levels related to question types do not vary greatly (mean responses ranged from 2.75 for *A* students to 3.83 for *F* students), which suggests that although question-related anxiety exists, it is not dramatic.

An analysis of the data further indicates that low-anxiety questions (true/false, multiple-choice, matching) are format based, providing information and allowing students to select among options. In contrast, high-anxiety questions (listing, fill-in-the-blank, essay) are open-ended, requiring students to recall and arrange information on their own.

Test Questions   8

The results of this brief study are, of course, tentative and need to be reproduced with a larger, more comprehensive sample. However, the study does suggest the value of analyzing specific question formats because they can contribute in a small but significant way to overall test anxiety.

The discussion ends with a comment on the value of the study.

Test Questions 9

References

Hancock, D. R. (2001). Effects of test anxiety and evaluative threat on students' achievement and motivation. *The Journal of Educational Research, 94,* 284–290.

Nelson, J. S., Jayanthi, M., Epstein, M. H., & Bursuck, W. D. (2000). Student preferences for adaptations in classroom testing. *Remedial and Special Education, 21*(1), 41–52.

Schutz, P. A., Davis, H. A., & Schwanenflugel, P. J. (2002). Organization of concepts relevant to emotions and their regulation during test taking. *The Journal of Experimental Education, 70*(4), 316–342.

Spielberger, C. D., & Vagg, P. R. (Eds.). (1995). *Test anxiety: Theory, assessment and treatment.* Washington, DC: Taylor.

Swanson, S., & Howell, C. (1996). Test anxiety in adolescents with learning disabilities and behavior disorders. *Exceptional Children, 62,* 389–397.

Weiner, B. (1994). Integrating social and personal theories of achievement striving. *Review of Educational Research, 64,* 557–573.

Wigfield, A., & Eccles, J. S. (1989). Test anxiety in elementary and secondary school students. *Educational Psychologist, 24,* 159–183.

Zeidner, M. (1995a). Adaptive coping with test situations: A review of the literature. *Educational Psychologist, 30,* 123–133.

Zeidner, M. (1995b). Coping with examination stress: Resources, strategies, outcomes. *Anxiety, Stress, and Coping, 8,* 279–298.

Page numbers continue consecutively. The descriptive title is centered.

Italics are used, not underlining.

The entire list is alphabetized and double-spaced.

First lines are at the normal margin; subsequent lines are indented.

Names are repeated in subsequent entries.

Table 1

Overall Responses (Security to Insecurity) to Question Types

Question Type	Rating					
	1	2	3	4	5	6
Matching	25.8	30.3	23.6	11.2	3.4	5.6
True/False	31.4	25.8	24.7	13.5	3.4	1.1
Fill-in-the-Blank	2.2	10.1	22.5	13.5	27.0	24.6
Multiple-Choice	25.8	32.6	25.9	6.7	6.7	2.2
Listing	4.5	5.6	24.7	21.4	22.5	21.4
Essay	6.8	13.5	7.9	10.1	12.4	49.4

Page numbers continue consecutively.

Numbered tables appear on separate pages.

Ruled lines separate elements for easy reading.

Table 2

Mean Response to Questions: Overall and by Student Grade Categories

Table titles appear in italics.

Question Type	By Category					
	Overall	A	B	C	D	F
Matching	2.53	1.56	2.29	2.67	2.78	3.24
True/False	2.35	2.39	2.35	2.80	2.33	2.00
Fill-in-the-Blank	4.27	3.17	4.00	4.33	4.67	5.00
Multiple-Choice	2.43	2.06	2.12	2.73	2.67	2.57
Listing	4.16	3.67	3.71	4.33	4.22	4.76
Essay	4.56	3.67	4.00	4.53	5.00	5.43

Column spacing is adjusted for easy reading.

The label is
centered.

Figure cap-
tions appear
on a separate
page.

Figure Caption

Figure 1. Test anxiety survey.

Numbered
figures appear
on separate
pages.

Figure 1

Survey: Test Anxiety—Reactions to Kinds of Test
Questions

M   F

Grade Last Nine Weeks: A   B   C   D   F

Circle one response for each kind of test question:
1 means that you feel *comfortable/secure* with
these kinds of questions (you won't worry about
that part of the test); *6* means that you feel
uncomfortable/insecure with these question types
(you will worry about how you do on that part of
the test). Consider tests for all classes, not just
English.

		Secure		No Reaction		Insecure	
1. Matching	1	2	3	4	5	6
2. True/False	1	2	3	4	5	6
3. Fill-in-the-Blank	1	2	3	4	5	6
4. Multiple-Choice	1	2	3	4	5	6
5. Listing	1	2	3	4	5	6
6. Essay	1	2	3	4	5	6

Please share any comments you have about types
of test questions:

_____

_____

_____

Features of Poster Presentations

Whether given at a conference or in a classroom, poster presentations share a variety of features, which may be surprisingly simple or highly elaborate.

- *Display surface.* The simplest "poster" can be prepared on a standard 2-by-3-foot sheet of poster board, mounted for extra stability. Displayed on an easel for easy viewing, this kind of poster is most commonly presented in the classroom. More elaborate posters are prepared as free-standing displays, may include multiple display panels, and may be quite expensive to prepare. Such complex posters are more common for presentations at large conferences.

- *Content.* To ensure that people focus properly on your work, create a clear and interesting title for the poster and provide identifying information about yourself (your name and affiliation). Because posters of all kinds must present content in concise, easily readable form, use headings judiciously. The standard divisions of a research paper—introduction, method, results, discussion, and others—provide familiar ways to divide the content of the poster, although other organizational patterns are also feasible.

- *Visual elements.* Because posters emphasize the visual presentation of research findings, use graphic elements to your advantage. Arrange information for easy interpretation, remembering that readers scan visual documents in the same way they read: from left to right and from top to bottom. When possible, reduce material to bulleted lists for easy scanning. Select simple fonts in sizes that can be read from 3 to 6 feet away. Use tables, charts, graphs, and images to clarify ideas. Employ color, when possible, to create visual interest.

- *Supporting documents.* Provide a one- to two-page supporting document that summarizes the information presented on your poster. Label it clearly with the presentation's title, provide your identifying information, and include key elements from the poster. Make copies for those attending the conference or for class members.

- *Presentation.* The poster does not stand on its ow rather, you must facilitate its review. Without sim reading or summarizing the material for your audience (after all, they can do that), highlight key features and direct their attention to the most salient points. Also, be prepared to answer questions and anticipate discussion.

Suggestions for Poster Presentations

Because the poster presentation is a unique format for presenting research, a well-planned presentation takes time to prepare and requires unique kinds of effort. Consider these suggestions:

- *Allow yourself sufficient time.* Do not assume that a poster session is easy to prepare. Not only does it require initial research, but it also warrants specialized preparation that may be new to you if you are used to preparing only written documents. Also, because the presentation includes more kinds of elements—visual and speaking components, as well as written content—preparing the poster presentation should not be a rushed effort.

- *Experiment with design elements.* Explore alternative ways to design your poster. Prepare material in several formats (try different fonts and font sizes; use different color combinations; prepare figures as tables *and* charts), and then decide which creates the best visual effect.

- *Solicit reactions.* Seek responses to your work from fellow students. Ask for overall reactions but also ask specific questions about presentational elements. If you have prepared alternative versions of your poster, ask which is most effective.

- *Practice your presentation.* Although a well-prepared poster should in some regards "speak for itself," consider the ways in which you can help an audience review your poster. Develop a set of "talking points," a brief list of comments to guide your explanations. When possible, practice your presentation with friends to ensure that your expression is clear and helpful.

- *Anticipate questions.* Think critically and predict questions that your audience might pose; then practice responding to those questions.

Abrams	Harry N. Abrams, Inc.
Acad. for Ed. Dev.	Academy for Educational Development, Inc.
ALA	American Library Association
Allen	George Allen and Unwin Publishers, Inc.
Allyn	Allyn and Bacon, Inc.
Appleton	Appleton-Century-Crofts
Ballantine	Ballantine Books, Inc.
Bantam	Bantam Books, Inc.
Barnes	Barnes and Noble Books
Basic	Basic Books
Beacon	Beacon Press, Inc.
Benn	Ernest Benn, Ltd.
Bobbs	The Bobbs-Merrill Co., Inc.
Bowker	R. R. Bowker Co.
CAL	Center for Applied Linguistics
Clarendon	Clarendon Press
Dell	Dell Publishing Co., Inc.
Dodd	Dodd, Mead, and Co.
Doubleday	Doubleday and Co., Inc.
Dover	Dover Publications, Inc.
Dutton	E. P. Dutton, Inc.
Einaudi	Giulio Einaudi Editore
Farrar	Farrar, Straus, and Giroux, Inc.
Feminist	The Feminist Press of the City University of New York
Free	The Free Press
Funk	Funk and Wagnalls, Inc.
Gale	Gale Research Co.
Gerig	Gerig Verlag
GPO	Government Printing Office
Harcourt	Harcourt Brace Jovanovich, Inc.
Harper	Harper and Row Publishers, Inc.
Harvard Law Rev. Assn.	Harvard Law Review Association
Heath	D. C. Heath and Co.
HMSO	Her (His) Majesty's Stationery Office

Holt	Holt, Rinehart, and Winston, Inc.
Houghton	Houghton Mifflin Co.
Humanities	Humanities Press, Inc.
Knopf	Alfred A. Knopf, Inc.
Larousse	Librairie Larousse
Lippincott	J. B. Lippincott Co.
Little	Little, Brown, and Co.
Macmillan	Macmillan Publishing Co., Inc.
McGraw	McGraw-Hill, Inc.
MLA	The Modern Language Association of America
NAL	The New American Library, Inc.
NCTE	The National Council of Teachers of English
NEA	The National Education Association
New York Graphic Soc.	New York Graphic Society
Norton	W. W. Norton and Co., Inc.
Penguin	Penguin Books, Inc.
Pocket	Pocket Books
Popular	The Popular Press
Prentice	Prentice-Hall, Inc.
PUF	Presses Universitaires de France
Putnam's	G. P. Putnam's Sons
Rand	Rand McNally and Co.
Random	Random House, Inc.
Rizzoli	Rizzoli Editore
St. Martin's	St. Martin's Press, Inc.
Scott	Scott, Foresman, and Co.
Scribner's	Charles Scribner's Sons
Simon	Simon and Schuster, Inc.
UMI	University Microfilms International
Viking	The Viking Press, Inc.

Index

Format for APA Reference-List Entries

1. Begin the first line at the left margin and indent subsequent lines one-half inch.
2. Invert the author's name so that the last name appears first; use first and middle initials.
3. When no author is named, list the source by title.
4. Place the publication date in parentheses, followed by a period.
5. Cite the complete title, including subtitles.
6. Use periods and one space to separate author, date, title, and publication information.

See pages 59–109 for additional information and examples.

Sample Reference-List Entries

An Article in a Journal with Continuous Paging
Nussbaum, J. F., & Bettini, L. M. (1994). Shared stories of the grandparent-grandchild relationship. *The International Journal of Aging and Human Development, 39*, 67–80.

An Article in a Journal with Separate Paging
Graves, D. (2000). Multiculturalism and the choral canon: 1975–2000. *Choral Journal, 41(2)*, 37–44.

An Article in a Monthly Magazine
Furlow, B. (2000, October). The uses of crying and begging. *Natural History, 109*, 62–67.

An Article in a Newspaper
Zeleny, J. (2000, January 17). Election reform is popular, political—and pricey. *The Chicago Tribune*, p. 2:1.

A Book by One Author
Monmonier, M. (1999). *Air apparent: How meteorologists learned to map, predict, and dramatize weather.* Chicago: University of Chicago Press.